ΕΥΡΙΠΙΔΟΥ EURIPIDES'

Ἠλέκτρα *Electra*

A Dual Language Edition

Greek Text Edited by
Gilbert Murray

English Translation and Notes by
Ian Johnston

Edited by
Evan Hayes and Stephen Nimis

FAENUM PUBLISHING
OXFORD, OHIO

Euripides Electra: *A Dual Language Edition*
First Edition

© 2015 by Faenum Publishing

ISBN-10: 194099716X
ISBN-13: 9781940997162

Published by Faenum Publishing, Ltd.
Cover Design: Evan Hayes

for Geoffrey (1974-1997)

οἵη περ φύλλων γενεὴ τοίη δὲ καὶ ἀνδρῶν.
φύλλα τὰ μέν τ᾽ ἄνεμος χαμάδις χέει, ἄλλα δέ θ᾽ ὕλη
τηλεθόωσα φύει, ἔαρος δ᾽ ἐπιγίγνεται ὥρῃ:
ὣς ἀνδρῶν γενεὴ ἣ μὲν φύει ἣ δ᾽ ἀπολήγει.

Generations of men are like the leaves.
In winter, winds blow them down to earth,
but then, when spring season comes again,
the budding wood grows more. And so with men:
one generation grows, another dies away.   (*Iliad* 6)

TABLE OF CONTENTS

EDITORS' NOTE

This volume presents the Ancient Greek text of Euripides' *Electra* with a facing English translation. The Greek text is that of Gilbert Murray (1913), from the Oxford Classical Texts series, which is in the public domain and available as a pdf. This text has also been digitized by the Perseus Project (perseus.tufts.edu). The English translation and accompanying notes are those of Ian Johnston of Vancouver Island University, Nanaimo, BC. This translation is available freely online (records.viu.ca/~johnstoi/). We have reset both texts, making a number of very minor corrections and modifications, and placed them on opposing pages. This facing-page format will be useful to those wishing to read the English translation while looking at version of the Greek original, or vice versa.

Occasionally readings from other editions of or commentaries on Euripides' Greek text are used, accounting for some minor departures from Murray. Even so, some small discrepancies exist between the Greek text and the English translation.

The House of Atreus:
A Note on the Mythological Background to the *Oresteia*
by Ian Johnston

Introduction

The following paragraphs provide a brief summary of the major events in the long history of the House of Atreus, one of the most fecund and long-lasting of all the Greek legends. Like so many other stories, the legend of the House of Atreus varies a good deal from one author to the next and there is no single authoritative version. The account given below tries to include as many of the major details as possible. At the end there is a short section reviewing Aeschylus' treatment of the story in the *Oresteia*.

Family Tree (Simplified)

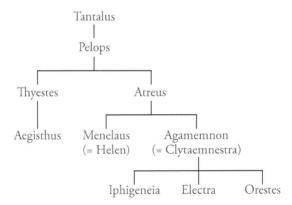

1. The family of Atreus (father of Agamemnon and Menelaus) traces its origins back to Tantalus, king of Sipylos, a son of Zeus (famous for his eternal punishment in Hades, as described in the *Odyssey*, where he is always thirsty but can never drink, hence the origin of the word *tantalizing*). Tantalus had a son called Pelops, whom Poseidon loved.

2. Pelops wished to marry Hippodameia, daughter of king Oenomaus. Oenomaus set up a contest (a chariot race against the king) for all those who wished to woo his daughter. If the suitor lost, he was killed. A number of men had died in such a race before Pelops made his attempt. Pelops bribed the king's charioteer (Myrtilus) to disable the king's chariot. In the race, Oenomaus' chariot broke down

(the wheels came off), and the king was killed. Pelops then carried off Hippodameia as his bride. Pelops also killed his co-conspirator Myrtilus by throwing him into the sea. Before he drowned Myrtilus (in some versions Oenomaus) cursed Pelops and his family. This act is the origin of the famous curse on the House of Atreus.

3. Pelops does not seems to have been affected by the curse. He had a number of children, the most important of whom were his two sons, the brothers Atreus and Thyestes. Atreus married Aerope, and they had two sons, Agamemnon and Menelaus. And Thyestes had two sons and a daughter Pelopia.

4. Atreus and Thyestes quarrelled (in some versions at the instigation of the god Hermes, father of Myrtilus, the charioteer killed by Pelops). Thyestes had an affair with Atreus' wife, Aerope, and was banished from Argos by Atreus. However, Thyestes petitioned to be allowed to return, and Atreus, apparently wishing a reconciliation, agreed to allow Thyestes to come back and prepared a huge banquet to celebrate the end of their differences.

5. At the banquet, however, Atreus served Thyestes the cooked flesh of Thyestes' two slaughtered sons. Thyestes ate the food, and then was informed of what he had done. This horrific event is the origin of the term *Thyestean Banquet*. Overcome with horror, Thyestes cursed the family of Atreus and left Argos with his one remaining child, his daughter Pelopia.

6. Some versions of the story include the name Pleisthenes, a son of Atreus who was raised by Thyestes. To become king, Thyestes sent Pleisthenes to kill Atreus, but Atreus killed him, not realizing he was killing his son. This, then, becomes another cause of the quarrel. In yet other accounts, someone called Pleisthenes is the first husband of Aerope and the father of Agamemnon and Menelaus. When he died, so this version goes, Atreus married Aerope and adopted her two sons. In Aeschylus' play there is one reference to Pleisthenes; otherwise, this ambiguous figure is absent from the story.

7. In some versions, including Aeschylus' account, Thyestes had one small infant son who survived the banquet, Aegisthus. In other accounts, however, Aegisthus was the product of Thyestes' incestuous relationship with his daughter Pelopia after the murder of the two older sons, conceived especially to be the avenger of the notorious banquet.

8. Agamemnon and Menelaus, the two sons of Atreus, married Clytaemnestra and Helen respectively, two twin sisters, but not identical twins (Clytaemnestra had a human father; whereas, Helen was a

daughter of Zeus). Helen was so famous for her beauty that a number of men wished to marry her. The suitors all agreed that they would act to support the man she eventually married in the event of any need for mutual assistance. Agamemnon and Clytaemnestra had three children, Iphigeneia, Orestes, and Electra.

9. When Helen (Menelaus' wife) ran off to Troy with Paris, Agamemnon and Menelaus organized and led the Greek forces against the Trojans. The army assembled at Aulis, but the fleet could not sail because of contrary winds sent by Artemis. Agamemnon sacrificed his daughter Iphigeneia in order to placate Artemis.

10. With Agamemnon and Menelaus off in Troy, Aegisthus (son of Thyestes) returned to Argos, where he became the lover of Clytaemnestra, Agamemnon's wife. They sent Orestes into exile, to live with an ally, Strophius in Phocis, and humiliated Electra, Agamemnon's surviving daughter (either treating her as a servant or marrying her off to a common farmer). When Agamemnon returned, the two conspirators successfully killed him and assumed royal control of Argos.

11. Orestes returned from exile and, in collaboration with his sister Electra, avenged his father by killing Clytaemnestra and Aegisthus. In many versions this act makes him lose his self-control and he becomes temporarily deranged. He then underwent ritual purification by Apollo and sought refuge in the temple of Athena in Athens. There he was tried and acquitted. This action put the curses placed on the House of Atreus to rest.

Some Comments

The story of the House of Atreus, and particularly Orestes' and Electra's revenge for their father's murder, is one of the most popular and enduring of all Greek legends, a favourite among the classical tragedians and still very popular with modern playwrights (e.g., T. S. Eliot, Eugene O'Neill, Jean Paul Sartre). However, different writers tell the story in very different ways.

Homer, for example (in the *Odyssey*) sets up Orestes' killing of Aegisthus as an entirely justified way to proceed (Homer ascribes the main motivation and planning to Aegisthus, who has to persuade Clytaemnestra to agree and who, it seems, does the actual killing). In fact, the action is repeatedly mentioned as a clear indication of divinely supported justice (there is no direct mention of the killing of Clytaemnestra, although there is a passing reference to Orestes' celebrations over his "hateful" mother after the killing of Aegisthus). Sophocles and Euripides tell basically the same story but with enormously different depictions of the main characters (in Euripides' version Orestes and Electra are hateful; whereas, in Sophocles' *Electra* they are much more conventionally righteous).

Aeschylus confines his attention to Atreus' crime against his brother (the Thyestean banquet) and what followed from it. There is no direct reference to Thyestes' adultery with Atreus' wife (although Cassandra makes a reference to a man sleeping with his brother's wife) or to any events from earlier parts of the story (unless the images of chariot racing are meant to carry an echo of Pelops' actions). This has the effect of making Atreus' crime against his brother the origin of the family curse (rather than the actions of Pelops or Tantalus) and tends to give the reader more sympathy for Aegisthus than some other versions do.

Curiously enough, Orestes' story has many close parallels with the Norse legend on which the story of Hamlet is based (son in exile is called upon to avenge a father killed by the man who has seduced his mother, perhaps with the mother's consent; the son carries out the act of killing his mother and her lover with great difficulty, undergoing fits of madness, and so on). Given that there is no suggestion of any possible literary-historical link between the origin of these two stories, the similarity of these plots offers a number of significant problems for psychologists and mythologists to explore. This puzzle is especially intriguing because the Hamlet-Orestes narrative is by far the most popular story in the history of English dramatic tragedy.

ΗΛΕΚΤΡΑ

ELECTRA

ΤΑ ΤΟΥ ΔΡΑΜΑΤΟΣ ΠΡΟΣΩΠΑ

ΑΥΤΟΥΡΓΟΣ ΜΥΚΗΝΑΙΟΣ

ΗΛΕΚΤΡΑ

ΟΡΕΣΤΗΣ

ΠΥΛΑΔΗΣ

ΧΟΡΟΣ

ΠΡΕΣΒΥΣ

ΑΓΓΕΛΟΣ

ΚΛΥΤΑΙΜΝΗΣΤΡΑ

ΔΙΟΣΚΟΥΡΟΙ

DRAMATIS PERSONAE

PEASANT: a poor farmer in the countryside

ELECTRA: daughter of Agamemnon and Clytaemnestra, married to the Peasant

ORESTES: son of Agamemnon and Clytaemnestra, brother of Electra

PYLADES: a friend of Orestes

CHORUS: Argive country women

OLD MAN: an old servant of Agamemnon's who rescued Orestes

MESSENGER: one of Orestes' servants

CLYTAEMNESTRA: mother of Orestes and Electra.

DIOSCOURI (Castor and Polydeuces): divine twin brothers of Helen and Clytaemnestra

SERVANTS: attendants for Orestes, Pylades, and Clytaemnestra

Ἠλέκτρα

ΑΥΤΟΥΡΓΟΣ
 Ὦ γῆς παλαιὸν ἄργος, Ἰνάχου ῥοαί,
ὅθεν ποτ' ἄρας ναυσὶ χιλίαις Ἄρη
ἐς γῆν ἔπλευσε Τρωάδ' Ἀγαμέμνων ἄναξ.
κτείνας δὲ τὸν κρατοῦντ' ἐν Ἰλιάδι χθονὶ
Πρίαμον, ἑλών τε Δαρδάνου κλεινὴν πόλιν,   5
ἀφίκετ' ἐς τόδ' Ἄργος, ὑψηλῶν δ' ἐπὶ
ναῶν ἔθηκε σκῦλα πλεῖστα βαρβάρων.
κἀκεῖ μὲν εὐτύχησεν· ἐν δὲ δώμασι
θνῄσκει γυναικὸς πρὸς Κλυταιμήστρας δόλῳ
καὶ τοῦ Θυέστου παιδὸς Αἰγίσθου χερί.   10
χὠ μὲν παλαιὰ σκῆπτρα Ταντάλου λιπὼν
ὄλωλεν, Αἴγισθος δὲ βασιλεύει χθονός,
ἄλοχον ἐκείνου Τυνδαρίδα κόρην ἔχων.
οὓς δ' ἐν δόμοισιν ἔλιφ' ὅτ' ἐς Τροίαν ἔπλει,
ἄρσενά τ' Ὀρέστην θῆλύ τ' Ἠλέκτρας θάλος,   15
τὸν μὲν πατρὸς γεραιὸς ἐκκλέπτει τροφεὺς
μέλλοντ' Ὀρέστην χερὸς ὑπ' Αἰγίσθου θανεῖν
Στροφίῳ τ' ἔδωκε Φωκέων ἐς γῆν τρέφειν·
ἣ δ' ἐν δόμοις ἔμεινεν Ἠλέκτρα πατρός,
ταύτην ἐπειδὴ θαλερὸς εἶχ' ἥβης χρόνος,   20
μνηστῆρες ᾔτουν Ἑλλάδος πρῶτοι χθονός.
δείσας δὲ μή τῳ παῖδ' ἀριστέων τέκοι
Ἀγαμέμνονος ποινάτορ', εἶχεν ἐν δόμοις
Αἴγισθος οὐδ' ἥρμοζε νυμφίῳ τινί.
ἐπεὶ δὲ καὶ τοῦτ' ἦν φόβου πολλοῦ πλέων,   25

Electra

PEASANT

O this old land, these streams of Inachus,
the place from where king Agamemnon once
set out with a thousand ships on his campaign
and sailed off over to the land of Troy.
He killed Priam, who ruled in Ilionk
and took the famous town of Dardanus.[1]
Then he returned home, back here to Argos,
and set up in high temples piles of loot
from those barbarians. Yes, over there
things went well for him. But then he was killed
in his own home, thanks to the treachery
of his wife, Clytaemnestra, at the hand   [10]
of Thyestes' son Aegisthus. So he died,
leaving behind Tantalus' ancient sceptre.[2]
Aegisthus rules this country now. He wed
Tyndareus' daughter, the dead king's wife.
As for those he left at home behind him
when he sailed to Troy, his son Orestes
and his daughter, too, Electra—well, now,
Aegisthus was about to kill Orestes,
but an old servant of his father's took him
and handed him to Strophius to bring up
in the land of Phocis. But Electra
stayed on in her father's house. When she reached
her young maturity, the suitors came,   [20]
the foremost ones throughout the land of Greece,
seeking marriage. Aegisthus was afraid
she'd bear a child to some important man,
who'd then seek revenge for Agamemnon.
So he wouldn't give her to a bridegroom,
but kept her in his home. Even this choice
filled him with fear, in case she'd give birth

5

μή τῳ λαθραίως τέκνα γενναίῳ τέκοι,
κτανεῖν σφε βουλεύσαντος, ὠμόφρων ὅμως
μήτηρ νιν ἐξέσωσεν Αἰγίσθου χερός.
ἐς μὲν γὰρ ἄνδρα σκῆψιν εἶχ' ὀλωλότα,
παίδων δ' ἔδεισε μὴ φθονηθείη φόνῳ.   30
ἐκ τῶνδε δὴ τοιόνδ' ἐμηχανήσατο
Αἴγισθος· ὃς μὲν γῆς ἀπηλλάχθη φυγὰς
Ἀγαμέμνονος παῖς, χρυσὸν εἰφ' ὃς ἂν κτάνῃ,
ἡμῖν δὲ δὴ δίδωσιν Ἠλέκτραν ἔχειν
δάμαρτα, πατέρων μὲν Μυκηναίων ἄπο   35
γεγῶσιν—οὐ δὴ τοῦτό γ' ἐξελέγχομαι·
λαμπροὶ γὰρ ἐς γένος γε, χρημάτων δὲ δὴ
πένητες, ἔνθεν ηὐγένει' ἀπόλλυται—
ὡς ἀσθενεῖ δοὺς ἀσθενῆ λάβοι φόβον.
εἰ γάρ νιν ἔσχεν ἀξίωμ' ἔχων ἀνήρ,   40
εὕδοντ' ἂν ἐξήγειρε τὸν Ἀγαμέμνονος
φόνον δίκη τ' ἂν ἦλθεν Αἰγίσθῳ τότε.
ἣν οὔποθ' ἀνὴρ ὅδε—σύνοιδέ μοι Κύπρις—
ᾔσχυνεν εὐνῇ· παρθένος δ' ἔτ' ἐστὶ δή.
αἰσχύνομαι γὰρ ὀλβίων ἀνδρῶν τέκνα   45
λαβὼν ὑβρίζειν, οὐ κατάξιος γεγώς.
στένω δὲ τὸν λόγοισι κηδεύοντ' ἐμοὶ
ἄθλιον Ὀρέστην, εἴ ποτ' εἰς Ἄργος μολὼν
γάμους ἀδελφῆς δυστυχεῖς ἐσόψεται.
ὅστις δέ μ' εἶναί φησι μῶρον, εἰ λαβὼν   50
νέαν ἐς οἴκους παρθένον μὴ θιγγάνω,
γνώμης πονηροῖς κανόσιν ἀναμετρούμενος
τὸ σῶφρον, ἴστω καὐτὸς αὖ τοιοῦτος ὤν.

ΗΛΕΚΤΡΑ
ὦ νὺξ μέλαινα, χρυσέων ἄστρων τροφέ,
ἐν ᾗ τόδ' ἄγγος τῷδ' ἐφεδρεῦον κάρα   55
φέρουσα πηγὰς ποταμίας μετέρχομαι—

to a noble child in secret. So he planned
to kill her. But though her heart is savage,
her mother saved her from Aegisthus' hands.
She'd an excuse for murdering her husband,
but she feared that if she killed her children   [30]
she'd be totally disgraced.³ And that's why
Aegisthus came up with the following scheme—
he offered gold to anyone who'd kill
Agamemnon's son, who'd left the country
as an exile, and he gave Electra
to me to be my wife. My ancestors
were from Mycenae, so in this matter
at least I don't bear any of the blame.
My family was a good one but not rich,
and that destroys one's noble ancestry.
He gave her to a man who had no power.
In that way his fear could be diminished.
If some important fellow married her,   [40]
he might have woken up the sleeping blood
of Agamemnon, and then at some point
justice would have come here for Aegisthus.
But I've never had sex with her in bed—
and Cypris knows I'm right in this—and so
Electra's still a virgin.⁴ I'd be ashamed
to take the daughter of a wealthy man
and violate the girl, when I'm not born
her equal. As for unfortunate Orestes,
who's now, according to what people say,
a relative of mine, I'm sorry for him,
if he should ever come back to Argos
and see his sister's wretched marriage.
Any man who says I'm just an idiot   [50]
to bring a young girl here into my home
and then not touch her should know he's a fool,
measuring wisdom with a useless standard.

[Electra enters from the hut. She is carrying a water jug]

ELECTRA
　　O pitch black night, nurse of golden stars,
　　Through you I walk towards the river streams,
　　holding up this jar I carry on my head.

οὐ δή τι χρείας ἐς τοσόνδ' ἀφιγμένη,
ἀλλ' ὡς ὕβριν δείξωμεν Αἰγίσθου θεοῖς —
γόους τ' ἀφίημ' αἰθέρ' ἐς μέγαν πατρί.
ἡ γὰρ πανώλης Τυνδαρίς, μήτηρ ἐμή,   60
ἐξέβαλέ μ' οἴκων, χάριτα τιθεμένη πόσει·
τεκοῦσα δ' ἄλλους παῖδας Αἰγίσθῳ πάρα
πάρεργ' Ὀρέστην κἀμὲ ποιεῖται δόμων . . .

ΑΥΤΟΥΡΓΟΣ

τί γὰρ τάδ', ὦ δύστην', ἐμὴν μοχθεῖς χάριν
πόνους ἔχουσα, πρόσθεν εὖ τεθραμμένη,   65
καὶ ταῦτ' ἐμοῦ λέγοντος οὐκ ἀφίστασαι;

ΗΛΕΚΤΡΑ

ἐγώ σ' ἴσον θεοῖσιν ἡγοῦμαι φίλον·
ἐν τοῖς ἐμοῖς γὰρ οὐκ ἐνύβρισας κακοῖς.
μεγάλη δὲ θνητοῖς μοῖρα συμφορᾶς κακῆς
ἰατρὸν εὑρεῖν, ὡς ἐγὼ σὲ λαμβάνω.   70
δεῖ δή με κἀκέλευστον εἰς ὅσον σθένω
μόχθου 'πικουφίζουσαν, ὡς ῥᾷον φέρῃς,
συνεκκομίζειν σοι πόνους. ἅλις δ' ἔχεις
τἄξωθεν ἔργα· τἀν δόμοις δ' ἡμᾶς χρεὼν
ἐξευτρεπίζειν. εἰσιόντι δ' ἐργάτῃ   75
θύραθεν ἡδὺ τἄνδον εὑρίσκειν καλῶς.

ΑΥΤΟΥΡΓΟΣ

εἴ τοι δοκεῖ σοι, στεῖχε· καὶ γὰρ οὐ πρόσω
πηγαὶ μελάθρων τῶνδ'. ἐγὼ δ' ἅμ' ἡμέρᾳ
βοῦς εἰς ἀρούρας ἐσβαλὼν σπερῶ γύας.
ἀργὸς γὰρ οὐδεὶς θεοὺς ἔχων ἀνὰ στόμα   80
βίον δύναιτ' ἂν ξυλλέγειν ἄνευ πόνου.

This is not a task I am compelled to do,
but I will manifest to all the gods
Aegisthus' insolence, and I will send
into this great sky my sorrowing cries
out to my father. For my own mother,   [60]
that murderous daughter of Tyndareus,
in her desire to please her husband,
has cast me from my home. With Aegisthus
she's given birth to other children and thinks
Orestes and myself of no account
inside her house.

PEASANT

                    You unfortunate girl,
why do you work like this to give me help,
carrying out these chores? In earlier days,
you were nobly raised. Why don't you stop,
especially when I mention this to you?

ELECTRA

You're kind to me, and I consider you
the equal of the gods in that. For now,
when I'm in trouble, you don't demean me.
When human beings discover someone there
to soothe their miseries, as I have you,   [70]
then fate is doing something great for them.
So I should help you carry out the work
and give you some relief, to the extent
my strength permits, without you asking me,
so you can bear the load more easily.
There's work enough for you to do outside.
I should take care of things within the house.
It's nice when someone working out of doors
comes back in and finds things neat and tidy.

PEASANT

Well, if you think you should do it, then go.
The springs are no great distance from the house.
Once daylight comes, I'll drive the oxen out,
go to the farmlands, and then sow the fields.
No matter how much his mouth talks of gods,   [80]
a lazy man can never gather up
the stuff he needs to live without hard work.

ΟΡΕΣΤΗΣ
Πυλάδη, σὲ γὰρ δὴ πρῶτον ἀνθρώπων ἐγὼ
πιστὸν νομίζω καὶ φίλον ξένον τ' ἐμοί·
μόνος δ' Ὀρέστην τόνδ' ἐθαύμαζες φίλων,
πράσσονθ' ἃ πράσσω δείν' ὑπ' Αἰγίσθου παθών,   85
ὅς μου κατέκτα πατέρα ... χἠ πανώλεθρος
μήτηρ. ἀφῖγμαι δ' ἐκ θεοῦ μυστηρίων
Ἀργεῖον οὖδας οὐδενὸς ξυνειδότος,
φόνον φονεῦσι πατρὸς ἀλλάξων ἐμοῦ.
νυκτὸς δὲ τῆσδε πρὸς τάφον μολὼν πατρὸς   90
δάκρυά τ' ἔδωκα καὶ κόμης ἀπηρξάμην
πυρᾷ τ' ἐπέσφαξ' αἷμα μηλείου φόνου,
λαθὼν τυράννους οἳ κρατοῦσι τῆσδε γῆς.
καὶ τειχέων μὲν ἐντὸς οὐ βαίνω πόδα,
δυοῖν δ' ἅμιλλαν ξυντιθεὶς ἀφικόμην   95
πρὸς τέρμονας γῆς τῆσδ', ἵν' ἐκβάλω ποδὶ
ἄλλην ἐπ' αἶαν, εἴ μέ τις γνοίη σκοπῶν,
ζητῶν τ' ἀδελφήν· φασὶ γάρ νιν ἐν γάμοις
ζευχθεῖσαν οἰκεῖν οὐδὲ παρθένον μένειν·
ὡς συγγένωμαι καὶ φόνου ξυνεργάτιν   100
λαβὼν τά γ' εἴσω τειχέων σαφῶς μάθω.
νῦν οὖν—Ἕως γὰρ λευκὸν ὄμμ' ἀναίρεται—
ἔξω τρίβου τοῦδ' ἴχνος ἀλλαξώμεθα.
ἢ γάρ τις ἀροτὴρ ἤ τις οἰκέτις γυνὴ
φανήσεται νῷν, ἥντιν' ἱστορήσομεν   105
εἰ τούσδε ναίει σύγγονος τόπους ἐμή.
ἀλλ'—εἰσορῶ γὰρ τήνδε πρόσπολόν τινα,
πηγαῖον ἄχθος ἐν κεκαρμένῳ κάρα
φέρουσαν—ἑζώμεσθα κἀκπυθώμεθα
δούλης γυναικός, ἤν τι δεξώμεσθ' ἔπος   110
ἐφ' οἷσι, Πυλάδη, τήνδ' ἀφίγμεθα χθόνα.

[Electra leaves for the spring, and the Peasant goes back to the house. Enter Orestes and Pylades, with two servants]

ORESTES

 Pylades, among men I think of you
 as a loving host, foremost in my trust.
 For you're the only one of all my friends
 who has dealt honourably with Orestes,
 as I've been coping with these dreadful things
 I've had to put up with from Aegisthus,
 who killed my father . . . he and my mother,
 that destructive woman. I've come here,
 from god's mysterious shrine to Argive lands,
 to avenge the killing of my father,
 by murdering the ones who butchered him.
 Last night I visited my father's tomb.   [90]
 where I wept and started sacrificing
 by cutting off a lock of hair. And then,
 on the altar I made an offering of blood
 from a sheep I slaughtered. But the tyrants
 who control this land don't know I'm here.
 I've not set foot within the city walls.
 No. I've come out to these border regions
 for two reasons which act on me as one—
 so I may run off to another land
 if someone sees me and knows who I am
 and to find my sister, who's living here,
 so they say, joined in marriage to a man,
 no virgin any more. I could meet her,   [100]
 make her my accomplice in the murder,
 and in this way get clear information
 about what's happening inside the walls.
 But now that Dawn is raising her bright eyes,
 let's move aside to some place off the path.
 We'll see a ploughman or a servant woman,
 then ask them if my sister lives near here.
 In fact, I can see a household servant—
 her shaven head holds up a water jug.⁵
 Let sit and ask this female slave some questions, [110]
 Pylades—see if we can get some word
 about the business which has brought us here.

ΗΛΕΚΤΡΑ
σύντειν'—ὥρα—ποδὸς ὁρμάν· ὤ,
ἔμβα, ἔμβα κατακλαίουσα·
    ἰώ μοί μοι.
  ἐγενόμαν Ἀγαμέμνονος   115
  καί μ' ἔτεκεν Κλυταιμήστρα
  στυγνὰ Τυνδάρεω κόρα,
  κικλήσκουσι δέ μ' ἀθλίαν
    Ἠλέκτραν πολιῆται.
  φεῦ φεῦ σχετλίων πόνων   120
    καὶ στυγερᾶς ζόας.
  ὦ πάτερ, σὺ δ' ἐν Ἀΐδα
  κεῖσαι, σᾶς ἀλόχου σφαγαῖς
    Αἰγίσθου τ', Ἀγάμεμνον.

ἴθι τὸν αὐτὸν ἔγειρε γόον,   125
ἄναγε πολύδακρυν ἁδονάν.

σύντειν'—ὥρα—ποδὸς ὁρμάν· ὤ,
ἔμβα, ἔμβα, κατακλαίουσα·
    ἰώ μοί μοι.
  τίνα πόλιν, τίνα δ' οἶκον, ὦ   130
  τλᾶμον σύγγον', ἀλατεύεις
  οἰκτρὰν ἐν θαλάμοις λιπὼν
  πατρῴοις ἐπὶ συμφοραῖς
    ἀλγίσταισιν ἀδελφάν;
  ἔλθοις τῶνδε πόνων ἐμοὶ   135
    τᾷ μελέᾳ λυτήρ,
  ὦ Ζεῦ Ζεῦ, πατρί θ' αἱμάτων
  ἐχθίστων ἐπίκουρος, Ἄρ-
    γει κέλσας πόδ' ἀλάταν.

θὲς τόδε τεῦχος ἐμῆς ἀπὸ κρατὸς ἑ-
λοῦσ', ἵνα πατρὶ γόους νυχίους   140
    ἐπορθροβοάσω,
  ἰαχάν, Ἀΐδα μέλος,

[Orestes and Pylades move back. Electra enters, on her way back from the spring. She does not see them at first. She starts to go through her ritual of mourning]

ELECTRA
>You must step quickly now —
>it's time to move —
>keep going, lamenting as you go.
>Alas for me! Yes, for me!
>I am Agamemnon's child.
>I was born from Clytaemnestra,
>Tyndareus' detested daughter.
>Miserable Electra — that's the name
>the citizens have given me.
>Alas, alas! My wretched work   [120]
>and this detested way of life!
>O father, you now lie in Hades,
>Agamemnon, thanks to that murder
>committed by Aegisthus and your wife.
>
>Come now, raise the same lament,
>seize the joy of prolonged weeping.
>
>You must step quickly now —
>it's time to move —
>keep going, lamenting as you go.
>Alas for me! Yes, for me!
>O my poor brother, in what town,   [130]
>in what household are you roaming,
>abandoning your abject sister
>to such painful circumstance
>in her ancestral home? Come to me,
>in my unhappy wretchedness.
>Be my deliverer from pain —
>ah Zeus, Zeus —
>be an avenger for my father,
>the hateful shedding of his blood,
>once the wanderer sets foot in Argos.
>
>Take this water pitcher from my head   [140]
>and set it down, so I may wail
>my night laments, cries for my father,

Ἀΐδα, πάτερ, σοι
κατὰ γᾶς ἐνέπω γόους
οἷς ἀεὶ τὸ κατ' ἦμαρ   145
διέπομαι, κατὰ μὲν φίλαν
ὄνυχι τεμνομένα δέραν
χέρα τε κρᾶτ' ἐπὶ κούριμον
τιθεμένα θανάτῳ σῷ.

    αἶ αἶ, δρύπτε κάρα·   150
οἷα δέ τις κύκνος ἀχέτας
ποταμίοις παρὰ χεύμασιν
πατέρα φίλτατον καλεῖ,
ὀλόμενον δολίοις βρόχων
ἔρκεσιν, ὡς σὲ τὸν ἄθλιον,   155
πάτερ, ἐγὼ κατακλαίομαι,
λουτρὰ πανύσταθ' ὑδρανάμενον χροῒ
κοίτᾳ ἐν οἰκτροτάτᾳ θανάτου.
    ἰώ μοι, ⟨ἰώ⟩ μοι
πικρᾶς μὲν πελέκεως τομᾶς   160
    σᾶς, πάτερ, πικρᾶς δ' ἐκ
Τροΐας ὁδίου βουλᾶς·
    οὐ μίτραισι γυνή σε
δέξατ' οὐδ' ἐπὶ στεφάνοις,
ξίφεσι δ' ἀμφιτόμοις λυγρὰν
Αἰγίσθου λώβαν θεμένα   165
    δόλιον ἔσχεν ἀκοίταν.

ΧΟΡΟΣ

    Ἀγαμέμνονος ὦ κόρα,
    ἤλυθον, Ἠλέκτρα, ποτὶ
        σὰν ἀγρότειραν αὐλάν.
ἔμολέ τις ἔμολεν γαλακτοπότας ἀνὴρ
    Μυκηναῖος ὀρειβάτας·   170
    ἀγγέλλει δ' ὅτι νῦν τριται-
    αν καρύσσουσιν θυσίαν
Ἀργεῖοι, πᾶσαι δὲ παρ' Ἥ-
ραν μέλλουσιν παρθενικαὶ στείχειν.

14

wild shrieks, a song of death,
your death, my father. For you
beneath the earth, I cry out
chants of sorrow—day after day
I keep up this constant grieving,
ripping my dear skin with my fingernails,
while my hand beats my shaven head—
all this because you're dead.

Ah yes, mutilate your face,   [150]
and, just as a swan sings out
beside the streaming river,
crying to its beloved father
who died ensnared within the web
of a deceitful net, so I cry out
for you, unhappy father,
your body bathing in that final bath,
your most pitiable couch of death.[6]

Ah me . . . ah me!
that bitter axe that hacked you,   [160]
father, the bitter scheme
of your return from Troy!
Your wife failed to welcome you
with victor's wreath and ribbons.
No. Instead she gave you up
to that disgraceful mutilation
by Aegisthus' two-edged sword
and got herself a treacherous mate.

[Enter the Chorus of Argive women]

CHORUS
    O Electra, daughter of Agamemnon,
    I've come here to your rural dwelling place.
    A man's arrived, a milk-drinking man—
    he's come here from Mycenae,   [170]
    a man who walks the mountains.
    He says the Argives have proclaimed
    a sacrifice two days from now,
    and every young bride has to go
    to Hera's shrine in the procession.

15

ΗΛΕΚΤΡΑ

οὐκ ἐπ' ἀγλαΐαις, φίλαι,   175
θυμὸν οὐδ' ἐπὶ χρυσέοις
  ὅρμοις ἐκπεπόταμαι
τάλαιν', οὐδ' ἱστᾶσα χοροὺς
  Ἀργείαις ἅμα νύμφαις
εἱλικτὸν κρούσω πόδ' ἐμόν.   180
  δάκρυσι νυχεύ-
ω, δακρύων δέ μοι μέλει
  δειλαίᾳ τὸ κατ' ἦμαρ.
σκέψαι μου πιναρὰν κόμαν
  καὶ τρύχη τάδ' ἐμῶν πέπλων,   15
εἰ πρέπουτ' Ἀγαμέμνονος
  κούρᾳ 'σται βασιλείᾳ
τᾷ Τροίᾳ θ', ἃ 'μοῦ πατέρος
  μέμναταί ποθ' ἁλοῦσα.

ΧΟΡΟΣ

μεγάλα θεός· ἀλλ' ἴθι,
καὶ παρ' ἐμοῦ χρῆσαι πολύ-   190
  πηνα φάρεα δῦναι,
χρύσεά τε—χαρίσαι—προσθήματ' ἀγλαΐας.
  δοκεῖς τοῖσι σοῖς δακρύοις
μὴ τιμῶσα θεούς, κρατή-
σειν ἐχθρῶν; οὔτοι στοναχαῖς,   195
  ἀλλ' εὐχαῖσι θεοὺς σεβί-
ζουσ' ἕξεις εὐαμερίαν, ὦ παῖ.

ΗΛΕΚΤΡΑ

οὐδεὶς θεῶν ἐνοπᾶς κλύει
  τᾶς δυσδαίμονος, οὐ παλαι-
ῶν πατρὸς σφαγιασμῶν.   200
οἴμοι τοῦ καταφθιμένου
  τοῦ τε ζῶντος ἀλάτα,
ὅς που γᾶν ἄλλαν κατέχει,
  μέλεος ἀλαί-
νων ποτὶ θῆσσαν ἑστίαν,   205
  τοῦ κλεινοῦ πατρὸς ἐκφύς.

16

ELECTRA

My sad heart is beating fast, my friends,
but not for festive ornaments
or necklaces made out of gold.
I won't stand with the Argive girls
in choruses or beat my foot
as I whirl in the dance.   [180]
I pass my days in tears—
in my unhappiness my care
day after day is with my tears.
See if this filthy hair and tattered clothes
suit Agamemnon's royal child
or Troy, which bears the memory
of how my father seized the place.

CHORUS

The goddess is great. So come,   [190]
borrow thick woven clothes from me
and put them on, with gold as well,
graceful ornaments—to favour me.
Do you think that with your tears
you can control your enemies
if you have no respect for gods?
My child, you'll find yourself a gentler life
by honouring the gods with prayers,
and not with sorrowful laments.

ELECTRA

No god is listening to the cries
of this ill-fated girl or to the murder
of my father all that time ago.   [200]
Alas for that slaughtered man
and for the wanderer still alive
dwelling somewhere in a foreign land,
a wretched vagabond at a slave's hearth,
son of such a famous father.

αὐτὰ δ' ἐν χερνῆσι δόμοις
ναίω ψυχὰν τακομένα
δωμάτων πατρίων φυγάς,
    οὐρείας ἀν' ἐρίπνας.   210

—   μάτηρ δ' ἐν λέκτροις φονίοις
    ἄλλῳ σύγγαμος οἰκεῖ.

ΧΟΡΟΣ

πολλῶν κακῶν Ἕλλησιν αἰτίαν ἔχει
σῆς μητρὸς Ἑλένη σύγγονος δόμοις τε σοῖς.

ΗΛΕΚΤΡΑ

οἴμοι, γυναῖκες, ἐξέβην θρηνημάτων.   215
ξένοι τινὲς παρ' οἶκον οἵδ' ἐφεστίους
εὐνὰς ἔχοντες ἐξανίστανται λόχου·
φυγῇ σὺ μὲν κατ' οἶμον, ἐς δόμους δ' ἐγὼ
φῶτας κακούργους ἐξαλύξωμεν ποδί.

ΟΡΕΣΤΗΣ

μέν', ὦ τάλαινα· μὴ τρέσῃς ἐμὴν χέρα.   220

ΗΛΕΚΤΡΑ

ὦ Φοῖβ' Ἄπολλον· προσπίτνω σε μὴ θανεῖν.

ΟΡΕΣΤΗΣ

ἄλλους κτάνοιμι μᾶλλον ἐχθίους σέθεν.

ΗΛΕΚΤΡΑ

ἄπελθε, μὴ ψαῦ' ὧν σε μὴ ψαύειν χρεών.

ΟΡΕΣΤΗΣ

οὐκ ἔσθ' ὅτου θίγοιμ' ἂν ἐνδικώτερον.

ΗΛΕΚΤΡΑ

καὶ πῶς ξιφήρης πρὸς δόμοις λοχᾷς ἐμοῖς;   225

ΟΡΕΣΤΗΣ

μείνασ' ἄκουσον, καὶ τάχ' οὐκ ἄλλως ἐρεῖς.

18

And I am living in a peasant's house,
wasting my soul up on the mountain tops
in exile from my father's house.   [210]
My mother, married to another man,
lives in a bed all stained with blood.

CHORUS LEADER

Your mother's sister, Helen, brought the Greeks
so many troubles and your house, as well.[7]

[Orestes and Pylades begin to move forward. Electra catches sight of them]

ELECTRA

Alas, women, I'll end my lamentation.
Some strangers hiding there beside the house,
at the altar, are rising up from ambush.
Let's run off—escape these trouble makers.
You run along the path. I'll go in the house.

ORESTES

Stay here, poor girl. Don't fear my hand.   [220]

ELECTRA

O Phoebus Apollo, I beseech you—
don't let me die!

ORESTES

                        And let me cut down
others I hate much more than you.

ELECTRA

                                    Leave now!
Don't put your hands on those you should not touch.

ORESTES

There's no one I have more right to touch.

ELECTRA

Then why wait beside my house in ambush,
with your sword drawn?

ORESTES

                        Stay here and listen.
Soon you'll be agreeing with me.

19

ΗΛΕΚΤΡΑ

ἕστηκα· πάντως δ' εἰμὶ σή· κρείσσων γὰρ εἶ.

ΟΡΕΣΤΗΣ

ἥκω φέρων σοι σοῦ κασιγνήτου λόγους.

ΗΛΕΚΤΡΑ

ὦ φίλτατ', ἆρα ζῶντος ἢ τεθνηκότος;

ΟΡΕΣΤΗΣ

ζῇ· πρῶτα γάρ σοι τἀγάθ' ἀγγέλλειν θέλω.   230

ΗΛΕΚΤΡΑ

εὐδαιμονοίης, μισθὸν ἡδίστων λόγων.

ΟΡΕΣΤΗΣ

κοινῇ δίδωμι τοῦτο νῷν ἀμφοῖν ἔχειν.

ΗΛΕΚΤΡΑ

ποῦ γῆς ὁ τλήμων τλήμονας φυγὰς ἔχων;

ΟΡΕΣΤΗΣ

οὐχ ἕνα νομίζων φθείρεται πόλεως νόμον.

ΗΛΕΚΤΡΑ

οὔ που σπανίζων τοῦ καθ' ἡμέραν βίου;   235

ΟΡΕΣΤΗΣ

ἔχει μέν, ἀσθενὴς δὲ δὴ φεύγων ἀνήρ.

ΗΛΕΚΤΡΑ

λόγον δὲ δὴ τίν' ἦλθες ἐκ κείνου φέρων;

ΟΡΕΣΤΗΣ

εἰ ζῇς, ὅπου τε ζῶσα συμφορᾶς ἔχεις.

ΗΛΕΚΤΡΑ

οὐκοῦν ὁρᾷς μου πρῶτον ὡς ξηρὸν δέμας.

ELECTRA

I'll stand here.
I'm yours, anyway, since you're the stronger.

ORESTES

I've come to bring you news about your brother.

ELECTRA

Dearest of friends — is he alive or dead?

ORESTES

Alive. I'd like you to have good news first.   [230]

ELECTRA

My you find happiness as your reward
for those most welcome words.

ORESTES

That's a blessing
I'd like to give to both of us together.

ELECTRA

My unhappy brother — in what country
does he live in wretched exile?

ORESTES

He drifts around,
not settling for a single city's customs.

ELECTRA

He's not lacking daily necessities?

ORESTES

No, those he has. But a man in exile
is truly powerless.

ELECTRA

What's the message
you've come here to bring from him?

ORESTES

I'm here
to see if you're alive and, if you are,
what your life is like.

ELECTRA

Surely you can see,
first of all, how my body's shrivelled?

Euripides

ΟΡΕΣΤΗΣ

λύπαις γε συντετηκός, ὥστε με στένειν. 240

ΗΛΕΚΤΡΑ

καὶ κρᾶτα πλόκαμόν τ᾽ ἐσκυθισμένον ξυρῷ.

ΟΡΕΣΤΗΣ

δάκνει σ᾽ ἀδελφὸς ὅ τε θανὼν ἴσως πατήρ.

ΗΛΕΚΤΡΑ

οἴμοι, τί γάρ μοι τῶνδέ γ᾽ ἐστὶ φίλτερον;

ΟΡΕΣΤΗΣ

φεῦ φεῦ· τί δαὶ σὺ σῷ κασιγνήτῳ, δοκεῖς;

ΗΛΕΚΤΡΑ

ἀπὼν ἐκεῖνος, οὐ παρὼν ἡμῖν φίλος. 245

ΟΡΕΣΤΗΣ

ἐκ τοῦ δὲ ναίεις ἐνθάδ᾽ ἄστεως ἑκάς;

ΗΛΕΚΤΡΑ

ἐγημάμεσθ᾽, ὦ ξεῖνε, θανάσιμον γάμον.

ΟΡΕΣΤΗΣ

ᾤμωξ᾽ ἀδελφὸν σόν. Μυκηναίων τίνι;

ΗΛΕΚΤΡΑ

οὐχ ᾧ πατήρ μ᾽ ἤλπιζεν ἐκδώσειν ποτέ.

ΟΡΕΣΤΗΣ

εἴφ᾽, ὡς ἀκούσας σῷ κασιγνήτῳ λέγω. 250

ΗΛΕΚΤΡΑ

ἐν τοῖσδ᾽ ἐκείνου τηλορὸς ναίω δόμοις.

ΟΡΕΣΤΗΣ

σκαφεύς τις ἢ βουφορβὸς ἄξιος δόμων.

22

ORESTES
> So worn with pain it makes me pity you.   [240]

ELECTRA
> And my hair cut off, shorn with a razor?

ORESTES
> Perhaps your dead father and your brother
> are tearing at you.

ELECTRA
>   Alas! Who is there
> whom I love more than those two men?

ORESTES
> Ah yes, and what do you think you are
> to your own brother?

ELECTRA
>   He's not here,
> and so no present friend to me.

ORESTES
>   Why live here,
> so distant from the city?

ELECTRA
>   I'm married —
> it's a deadly state.

ORESTES
>   I pity your brother.
> Did you marry someone from Mycenae?

ELECTRA
> No one my father ever hoped to give me.

ORESTES
> Tell me. I'll listen and inform your brother.   [250]

ELECTRA
> I live in his house, far from the city.

ORESTES
> This is a house fit for a ditch digger
> or for a herdsman.

ΗΛΕΚΤΡΑ

πένης ἀνὴρ γενναῖος ἔς τ' ἔμ' εὐσεβής.

ΟΡΕΣΤΗΣ

ἡ δ' εὐσέβεια τίς πρόσεστι σῷ πόσει;

ΗΛΕΚΤΡΑ

οὐπώποτ' εὐνῆς τῆς ἐμῆς ἔτλη θιγεῖν.   255

ΟΡΕΣΤΗΣ

ἅγνευμ' ἔχων τι θεῖον ἤ σ' ἀπαξιῶν;

ΗΛΕΚΤΡΑ

γονέας ὑβρίζειν τοὺς ἐμοὺς οὐκ ἠξίου.

ΟΡΕΣΤΗΣ

καὶ πῶς γάμον τοιοῦτον οὐχ ἥσθη λαβών;

ΗΛΕΚΤΡΑ

οὐ κύριον τὸν δόντα μ' ἡγεῖται, ξένε.

ΟΡΕΣΤΗΣ

ξυνῆκ'· Ὀρέστῃ μή ποτ' ἐκτείσῃ δίκην.   260

ΗΛΕΚΤΡΑ

τοῦτ' αὐτὸ ταρβῶν, πρὸς δὲ καὶ σώφρων ἔφυ.

ΟΡΕΣΤΗΣ

φεῦ·

γενναῖον ἄνδρ' ἔλεξας, εὖ τε δραστέον.   262

ΗΛΕΚΤΡΑ

εἰ δή ποθ' ἥξει γ' ἐς δόμους ὁ νῦν ἀπών.

ELECTRA

He's poor but decent,
and he respects me.

ORESTES

Your husband's respect —
what does that mean?

ELECTRA

Never once has he dared
to fondle me in bed.

ORESTES

Does he hold back
from some religious scruple, or does he think
you're unworthy of him?

ELECTRA

No. He believes
it's not right to insult my ancestors.

ORESTES

But how could he not be overjoyed
at making such a marriage?

ELECTRA

Well, stranger,
he thinks the person who gave me away
had no right to do it.

ORESTES

I understand.   [260]
He fears that someday he'll be punished
by Orestes.

ELECTRA

He is afraid of that,
but he's a virtuous man, as well.

ORESTES

Ah yes,
you've been talking of a noble man
who must be treated well.

ELECTRA

Yes, if the man
who's far away from here right now comes back.

ΟΡΕΣΤΗΣ

μήτηρ δέ σ᾽ ἡ τεκοῦσα ταῦτ᾽ ἠνέσχετο;

ΗΛΕΚΤΡΑ

γυναῖκες ἀνδρῶν, ὦ ξέν᾽, οὐ παίδων φίλαι.   265

ΟΡΕΣΤΗΣ

τίνος δέ σ᾽ οὕνεχ᾽ ὕβρισ᾽ Αἴγισθος τάδε;

ΗΛΕΚΤΡΑ

τεκεῖν μ᾽ ἐβούλετ᾽ ἀσθενῆ, τοιῷδε δούς.

ΟΡΕΣΤΗΣ

ὡς δῆθε παῖδας μὴ τέκοις ποινάτορας;

ΗΛΕΚΤΡΑ

τοιαῦτ᾽ ἐβούλευσ᾽· ὧν ἐμοὶ δοίη δίκην.

ΟΡΕΣΤΗΣ

οἶδεν δέ σ᾽ οὖσαν παρθένον μητρὸς πόσις;   270

ΗΛΕΚΤΡΑ

οὐκ οἶδε· σιγῇ τοῦθ᾽ ὑφαιρούμεσθά νιν.

ΟΡΕΣΤΗΣ

αἵδ᾽ οὖν φίλαι σοι τούσδ᾽ ἀκούουσιν λόγους;

ΗΛΕΚΤΡΑ

ὥστε στέγειν γε τἀμὰ καὶ σ᾽ ἔπη καλῶς.

ΟΡΕΣΤΗΣ

τί δῆτ᾽ Ὀρέστης πρὸς τόδ᾽, Ἄργος ἢν μόλῃ;

ΗΛΕΚΤΡΑ

ἤρου τόδ᾽; αἰσχρόν γ᾽ εἶπας· οὐ γὰρ νῦν ἀκμή;   275

ΟΡΕΣΤΗΣ

ἐλθὼν δὲ δὴ πῶς φονέας ἂν κτάνοι πατρός;

ORESTES

And your mother, the one who bore you,
how did she take this?

ELECTRA

Women give their love
to their husbands, stranger, not their children.

ORESTES

Why did Aegisthus shame you in this way?

ELECTRA

By giving me to such a man, he planned
the children I produced would not be strong.

ORESTES

Clearly so that you would not bear children
who could take revenge?

ELECTRA

Yes, that's his plan.
I hope he'll have to make that up to me!

ORESTES

You're a virgin — does your mother's husband know?   [270]

ELECTRA

No. We hide that from him with our silence.

ORESTES

These women listening to what we're saying
are friends of yours?

ELECTRA

Yes. They'll keep well concealed
my words and yours.

ORESTES

If he came to Argos
what could Orestes do in all of this?

ELECTRA

You have to ask? What a shameful question!
Isn't now a crucial time?

ORESTES

When he comes,
how should he kill his father's murderers?

ΗΛΕΚΤΡΑ

τολμῶν ὑπ᾽ ἐχθρῶν οἷ᾽ ἐτολμήθη πατήρ.

ΟΡΕΣΤΗΣ

ἦ καὶ μετ᾽ αὐτοῦ μητέρ᾽ ἂν τλαίης κτανεῖν;

ΗΛΕΚΤΡΑ

ταὐτῷ γε πελέκει τῷ πατὴρ ἀπώλετο.

ΟΡΕΣΤΗΣ

λέγω τάδ᾽ αὐτῷ, καὶ βέβαια τἀπὸ σοῦ;   280

ΗΛΕΚΤΡΑ

θάνοιμι μητρὸς αἷμ᾽ ἐπισφάξασ᾽ ἐμῆς.

ΟΡΕΣΤΗΣ

φεῦ·
εἴθ᾽ ἦν Ὀρέστης πλησίον κλύων τάδε.

ΗΛΕΚΤΡΑ

ἀλλ᾽, ὦ ξέν᾽, οὐ γνοίην ἂν εἰσιδοῦσά νιν.

ΟΡΕΣΤΗΣ

νέα γάρ, οὐδὲν θαῦμ᾽, ἀπεζεύχθης νέου.

ΗΛΕΚΤΡΑ

εἷς ἂν μόνος νιν τῶν ἐμῶν γνοίη φίλων.   285

ΟΡΕΣΤΗΣ

ἆρ᾽ ὃν λέγουσιν αὐτὸν ἐκκλέψαι φόνου;

ΗΛΕΚΤΡΑ

πατρός γε παιδαγωγὸς ἀρχαῖος γέρων.

ΟΡΕΣΤΗΣ

ὁ κατθανὼν δὲ σὸς πατὴρ τύμβου κυρεῖ;

ΗΛΕΚΤΡΑ

ἔκυρσεν ὡς ἔκυρσεν, ἐκβληθεὶς δόμων.

ELECTRA

By daring what my father's enemies
dared to do to him.

ORESTES

And would you dare
to help him kill your mother?

ELECTRA

Yes, I would—
with the very axe that killed our father!

ORESTES

Shall I tell him this? Are you quite certain?   [280]

ELECTRA

Once I've shed my mother's blood, let me die!

ORESTES

Ah, if only Orestes were close by
and could hear this!

ELECTRA

Stranger, if I saw him,
I would not know him.

ORESTES

That's not surprising.
You were youngsters when you separated.

ELECTRA

Only one of my friends would recognize him.

ORESTES

The man who they say saved him from murder
by stealing him away?

ELECTRA

Yes. An old man—
my father's servant long ago.

ORESTES

Your father—
when he died, did he get a burial tomb?

ELECTRA

Once he'd been thrown out of the house,
he found what he could find.

29

ΟΡΕΣΤΗΣ

οἴμοι, τόδ' οἷον εἶπας· . . . αἴσθησις γὰρ οὖν   290
κἀκ τῶν θυραίων πημάτων δάκνει βροτούς.
λέξον δ', ἵν' εἰδὼς σῷ κασιγνήτῳ φέρω
λόγους ἀτερπεῖς, ἀλλ' ἀναγκαίους κλύειν.
ἔνεστι δ' οἶκτος ἀμαθίᾳ μὲν οὐδαμοῦ,
σοφοῖσι δ' ἀνδρῶν· καὶ γὰρ οὐδ' ἀζήμιον   295
γνώμην ἐνεῖναι τοῖς σοφοῖς λίαν σοφήν.

ΧΟΡΟΣ

κἀγὼ τὸν αὐτὸν τῷδ' ἔρον ψυχῆς ἔχω.
πρόσω γὰρ ἄστεως οὖσα τἀν πόλει κακὰ
οὐκ οἶδα, νῦν δὲ βούλομαι κἀγὼ μαθεῖν.

ΗΛΕΚΤΡΑ

λέγοιμ' ἄν, εἰ χρή—χρὴ δὲ πρὸς φίλον λέγειν—   300
τύχας βαρείας τὰς ἐμὰς κἀμοῦ πατρός.
ἐπεὶ δὲ κινεῖς μῦθον, ἱκετεύω, ξένε,
ἄγγελλ' Ὀρέστῃ τἀμὰ καὶ κείνου κακά,
πρῶτον μὲν οἵοις ἐν πέπλοις αὐλίζομαι,
πίνῳ θ' ὅσῳ βέβριθ', ὑπὸ στέγαισί τε   305
οἵαισι ναίω βασιλικῶν ἐκ δωμάτων,
αὐτὴ μὲν ἐκμοχθοῦσα κερκίσιν πέπλους,
ἢ γυμνὸν ἕξω σῶμα κἀστερήσομαι,
αὐτὴ δὲ πηγὰς ποταμίους φορουμένη,
ἀνέορτος ἱερῶν καὶ χορῶν τητωμένη.   310
ἀναίνομαι γυναῖκας οὖσα παρθένος,
ἀναίνομαι δὲ Κάστορ', ᾧ πρὶν ἐς θεοὺς
ἐλθεῖν ἔμ' ἐμνήστευον, οὖσαν ἐγγενῆ.
μήτηρ δ' ἐμὴ Φρυγίοισιν ἐν σκυλεύμασιν
θρόνῳ κάθηται, πρὸς δ' ἕδραισιν Ἀσίδες   315
δμωαὶ στατίζουσ', ἃς ἔπερσ' ἐμὸς πατήρ,
Ἰδαῖα φάρη χρυσέαις ἐζευγμέναι
πόρπαισιν. αἷμα δ' ἔτι πατρὸς κατὰ στέγας
μέλαν σέσηπεν, ὃς δ' ἐκεῖνον ἔκτανεν,
ἐς ταὐτὰ βαίνων ἅρματ' ἐκφοιτᾷ πατρί,   320

ORESTES

                Alas! Those words of yours . . .   [290]
  Awareness even of a stranger's pains
  gnaws away at mortal men. Tell me this—
  once I know, I can carry to your brother
  the joyless story which he has to hear.
  Pity does not exist with ignorance,
  only with those who know. Too much knowledge
  is not without its dangers for wise men.

CHORUS LEADER

  My heart's desires are the same as his.
  Out here, far from the city, I don't know
  the troubles there. Now I want to hear them.

ELECTRA

  I will speak out, if that's acceptable—   [300]
  and it is appropriate to talk with friends
  about the burden of my situation
  and my father's. And I beg you, stranger,
  since you've the one who prompted me to speak,
  tell Orestes of our troubles, mine and his.
  First of all, there's the sort of clothes I wear,
  kept here in a stall, weighed down with filth.
  Then there's the style of house I'm living in,
  now I've been thrown out of my royal home.
  I have to work hard at the loom myself
  to make my clothes or else I'd have to go
  with my body naked—just do without,
  bringing water from the springs all by myself,
  with no share in the ritual festivals,   [310]
  no place in the dance. Since I'm a virgin,
  I keep married women at a distance
  and felt shamed by Castor, who courted me,
  his relative, before he joined the gods.[8]
  Meanwhile my mother sits there on her throne,
  with loot from Phrygia and Asian slaves,
  my father's plunder, standing by her chair,
  their Trojan dresses pinned with golden brooches.
  My father's blood still stains the palace walls—
  it's rotted black—while the man who killed him
  climbs in my father's chariot and drives out,   [320]

καὶ σκῆπτρ' ἐν οἷς Ἕλλησιν ἐστρατηλάτει
μιαιφόνοισι χερσὶ γαυροῦται λαβών.
Ἀγαμέμνονος δὲ τύμβος ἠτιμασμένος
οὔπω χοάς ποτ' οὐδὲ κλῶνα μυρσίνης
ἔλαβε, πυρὰ δὲ χέρσος ἀγλαϊσμάτων.   325
μέθῃ δὲ βρεχθεὶς τῆς ἐμῆς μητρὸς πόσις
ὁ κλεινός, ὡς λέγουσιν, ἐνθρῴσκει τάφῳ
πέτροις τε λεύει μνῆμα λάινον πατρός,
καὶ τοῦτο τολμᾷ τοὔπος εἰς ἡμᾶς λέγειν·
Ποῦ παῖς Ὀρέστης; ἆρά σοι τύμβῳ καλῶς   330
παρὼν ἀμύνει; — ταῦτ' ἀπὼν ὑβρίζεται.
ἀλλ', ὦ ξέν', ἱκετεύω σ', ἀπάγγειλον τάδε.
πολλοὶ δ' ἐπιστέλλουσιν, ἑρμηνεὺς δ' ἐγώ,
αἱ χεῖρες ἡ γλῶσσ' ἡ ταλαίπωρός τε φρήν,
κάρα τ' ἐμὸν ξυρῆκες, ὅ τ' ἐκεῖνον τεκών.   335
αἰσχρὸν γάρ, εἰ πατὴρ μὲν ἐξεῖλεν Φρύγας,
ὁ δ' ἄνδρ' ἕν' εἷς ὢν οὐ δυνήσεται κτανεῖν,
νέος πεφυκὼς κἀξ ἀμείνονος πατρός.

ΧΟΡΟΣ
καὶ μὴν δέδορκα τόνδε, σὸν λέγω πόσιν,
λήξαντα μόχθου πρὸς δόμους ὡρμημένον.   340

ΑΥΤΟΥΡΓΟΣ
ἔα· τίνας τούσδ' ἐν πύλαις ὁρῶ ξένους;
τίνος δ' ἕκατι τάσδ' ἐπ' ἀγραύλους πύλας
προσῆλθον; ἢ 'μοῦ δεόμενοι; γυναικί τοι
αἰσχρὸν μετ' ἀνδρῶν ἑστάναι νεανιῶν.

ΗΛΕΚΤΡΑ
ὦ φίλτατ', εἰς ὕποπτα μὴ μόλῃς ἐμοί·   345
τὸν ὄντα δ' εἴσῃ μῦθον· οἵδε γὰρ ξένοι
ἥκουσ' Ὀρέστου πρός με κήρυκες λόγων.
ἀλλ', ὦ ξένοι, σύγγνωτε τοῖς εἰρημένοις.

proud to brandish in his blood-stained hands
the very sceptre which my father used
to rule the Greeks. Agamemnon's grave
has not been honoured. It's had no libations,
no myrtle branch, its altar unadorned.
But this splendid husband of my mother,
so they say, when he's soaking wet with drink,
jumps on the grave and starts pelting pebbles
at the stone memorial to my father,
and dares to cry out these words against us:
"Where's your son Orestes? Is he present   [330]
to fight well for you and defend this tomb?"
And so absent Orestes is insulted.
But I beg you, stranger, take back this news.
Many are summoning him — I speak for them —
my hands and tongue, my grief-stricken heart,
my shaven head, and Agamemnon, too.
It would be disgraceful if his father
could destroy the Phrygians and yet he,
one against one, could not destroy a man,
when he's young and from a nobler father.

[Enter the Peasant, returning from the fields]

CHORUS LEADER

    Look! I see a man — I mean your husband —
    he's left his work. He's coming to the house.   [340]

PEASANT

    Hold on. Who are these strangers I see there,
    at the door? And why have they come here,
    to a farmer's gate? What do they want from me?
    It's shameful for a woman to be standing
    with young men.

ELECTRA

                My dear friend, don't suspect me.
    You'll hear what's going on. These strangers
    have come here from Orestes — they're messengers
    with news for me. But forgive him, strangers,
    for those words he said.

Euripides

ΑΥΤΟΥΡΓΟΣ

τί φασίν; ἀνὴρ ἔστι καὶ λεύσσει φάος;

ΗΛΕΚΤΡΑ

ἔστιν λόγῳ γοῦν, φασὶ δ' οὐκ ἄπιστ' ἐμοί.   350

ΑΥΤΟΥΡΓΟΣ

ἦ καί τι πατρὸς σῶν τε μέμνηται κακῶν;

ΗΛΕΚΤΡΑ

ἐν ἐλπίσιν ταῦτ'· ἀσθενὴς φεύγων ἀνήρ.

ΑΥΤΟΥΡΓΟΣ

ἦλθον δ' Ὀρέστου τίν' ἀγορεύοντες λόγον;

ΗΛΕΚΤΡΑ

σκοποὺς ἔπεμψε τούσδε τῶν ἐμῶν κακῶν.

ΑΥΤΟΥΡΓΟΣ

οὐκοῦν τὰ μὲν λεύσσουσι, τὰ δὲ σύ που λέγεις.   355

ΗΛΕΚΤΡΑ

ἴσασιν, οὐδὲν τῶνδ' ἔχουσιν ἐνδεές.

ΑΥΤΟΥΡΓΟΣ

οὐκοῦν πάλαι χρῆν τοῖσδ' ἀνεπτύχθαι πύλας;
χωρεῖτ' ἐς οἴκους· ἀντὶ γὰρ χρηστῶν λόγων
ξενίων κυρήσεθ', οἷ' ἐμὸς κεύθει δόμος.
αἴρεσθ', ὀπαδοί, τῶνδ' ἔσω τεύχη δόμων.   360
καὶ μηδὲν ἀντείπητε, παρὰ φίλου φίλοι
μολόντες ἀνδρός· καὶ γὰρ εἰ πένης ἔφυν,
οὔτοι τό γ' ἦθος δυσγενὲς παρέξομαι.

ΟΡΕΣΤΗΣ

πρὸς θεῶν, ὅδ' ἀνὴρ ὃς συνεκκλέπτει γάμους
τοὺς σούς, Ὀρέστην οὐ καταισχύνειν θέλων;   365

34

PEASANT

What are they saying?
Is the man still gazing at the daylight?

ELECTRA

That's what they say, and I believe their news.   [350]

PEASANT

Does he still recall your father's troubles
and your own?

ELECTRA

We can hope about those things,
but a man in exile has no power.

PEASANT

What message from Orestes did they bring
when they came here?

ELECTRA

He sent them out as spies
to look into my troubles.

PEASANT

They're seeing some,
and I suppose you're telling them the rest.

ELECTRA

They know—there's no shortage of them.

PEASANT

Surely we should have opened up our doors
long before this point. Go inside the house.
In exchange for your good news, you'll find
the hospitality my house affords.
You servants, take the stuff inside the house.   [360]
Do not refuse me—you are friends of ours
and you've come from someone who's a friend.
Even if I'm poor, I will not behave
like someone with an ill-bred character.

ORESTES

By the gods, is this the man pretending
you and he are married, who does not wish
to bring dishonour to Orestes?

35

ΗΛΕΚΤΡΑ

οὗτος κέκληται πόσις ἐμὸς τῆς ἀθλίας.

ΟΡΕΣΤΗΣ

φεῦ·
οὐκ ἔστ' ἀκριβὲς οὐδὲν εἰς εὐανδρίαν·
ἔχουσι γὰρ ταραγμὸν αἱ φύσεις βροτῶν.
ἤδη γὰρ εἶδον ἄνδρα γενναίου πατρὸς
τὸ μηδὲν ὄντα, χρηστά τ' ἐκ κακῶν τέκνα,   370
λιμόν τ' ἐν ἀνδρὸς πλουσίου φρονήματι,
γνώμην τε μεγάλην ἐν πένητι σώματι.
πῶς οὖν τις αὐτὰ διαλαβὼν ὀρθῶς κρινεῖ;
πλούτῳ; πονηρῷ τἄρα χρήσεται κριτῇ.
ἢ τοῖς ἔχουσι μηδέν; ἀλλ' ἔχει νόσον   375
πενία, διδάσκει δ' ἄνδρα τῇ χρείᾳ κακόν.
ἀλλ' εἰς ὅπλ' ἔλθω; τίς δὲ πρὸς λόγχην βλέπων
μάρτυς γένοιτ' ἂν ὅστις ἐστὶν ἀγαθός;
κράτιστον εἰκῇ ταῦτ' ἐᾶν ἀφειμένα.
οὗτος γὰρ ἀνὴρ οὔτ' ἐν Ἀργείοις μέγας   380
οὔτ' αὖ δοκήσει δωμάτων ὠγκωμένος,
ἐν τοῖς δὲ πολλοῖς ὤν, ἄριστος ηὑρέθη.
οὐ μὴ φρονήσεθ', οἳ κενῶν δοξασμάτων
πλήρεις πλανᾶσθε, τῇ δ' ὁμιλίᾳ βροτοὺς
κρινεῖτε καὶ τοῖς ἤθεσιν τοὺς εὐγενεῖς;   385
οἱ γὰρ τοιοῦτοι καὶ πόλεις οἰκοῦσιν εὖ
καὶ δώμαθ'· αἱ δὲ σάρκες αἱ κεναὶ φρενῶν
ἀγάλματ' ἀγορᾶς εἰσιν. οὐδὲ γὰρ δόρυ
μᾶλλον βραχίων σθεναρὸς ἀσθενοῦς μένει·
ἐν τῇ φύσει δὲ τοῦτο κἀν εὐψυχίᾳ.   390
ἀλλ'—ἄξιος γὰρ ὅ τε παρὼν ὅ τ' οὐ παρὼν
Ἀγαμέμνονος παῖς, οὗπερ οὕνεχ' ἥκομεν—
δεξώμεθ' οἴκων καταλύσεις. χωρεῖν χρεών,
δμῶες, δόμων τῶνδ' ἐντός. ὡς ἐμοὶ πένης
εἴη πρόθυμος πλουσίου μᾶλλον ξένος.   395

ELECTRA

He is—

    he's the one who in my miserable state
    they call my husband.

ORESTES

              Well, nothing is precise
    when it comes to how a man is valued—
    men's natures are confusing. Before this,
    I've seen a man worth nothing, yet he had   [370]
    a noble father, and evil parents
    with outstanding children. I've seen famine
    in a rich man's thinking and great spirit
    in a poor man's body. So how can we
    sort out these things and judge correctly?
    By riches? That would be a wretched test.
    By those who have nothing? But poverty
    is a disease. Through need it teaches men
    to act in evil ways. So should I turn
    to warfare? But when facing hostile spears,
    who can testify which men are virtuous?
    Best to dismiss such things, leave them to chance.
    This man is not great among the Argives,
    nor puffed up by his family's reputation.
    He's one of the crowd, yet has proved himself
    an excellent man. So stop your foolishness,
    those of you who keep wandering around
    full of misguided ways of measuring worth.
    Why not judge how valuable men are
    by their behaviour and their company?
    Men like this one govern homes and cities well,
    while those with muscles and with vacant minds
    are mere decorations in the market place.
    In fights with spears the strong arm holds its ground
    no better than the weak one does—such things
    depend on a man's nature and his courage.   [390]
    But because the man who is both absent
    and yet present here is worthy of it—
    I mean Agamemnon's son, for whose sake
    we've come here—let's accept the lodging
    in this home. You slaves, go inside the house.
    May a poor but willing man be my host

Euripides

αἰνῶ μὲν οὖν τοῦδ᾽ ἀνδρὸς ἐσδοχὰς δόμων,
ἐβουλόμην δ᾽ ἄν, εἰ κασίγνητός με σὸς
ἐς εὐτυχοῦντας ἦγεν εὐτυχῶν δόμους.
ἴσως δ᾽ ἂν ἔλθοι· Λοξίου γὰρ ἔμπεδοι
χρησμοί, βροτῶν δὲ μαντικὴν χαίρειν ἐῶ.   400

ΧΟΡΟΣ

νῦν ἢ πάροιθεν μᾶλλον, Ἠλέκτρα, χαρᾷ
θερμαινόμεσθα καρδίαν· ἴσως γὰρ ἂν
μόλις προβαίνουσ᾽ ἡ τύχη σταίη καλῶς.

ΗΛΕΚΤΡΑ

ὦ τλῆμον, εἰδὼς δωμάτων χρείαν σέθεν
τί τούσδ᾽ ἐδέξω μείζονας σαυτοῦ ξένους;   405

ΑΥΤΟΥΡΓΟΣ

τί δ᾽; εἴπερ εἰσὶν ὡς δοκοῦσιν εὐγενεῖς,
οὐκ ἔν τε μικροῖς ἔν τε μὴ στέρξουσ᾽ ὁμῶς;

ΗΛΕΚΤΡΑ

ἐπεί νυν ἐξήμαρτες ἐν σμικροῖσιν ὤν,
ἔλθ᾽ ὡς παλαιὸν τροφὸν ἐμοῦ φίλον πατρός,
ὃς ἀμφὶ ποταμὸν Τάναον Ἀργείας ὅρους   410
τέμνοντα γαίας Σπαρτιάτιδός τε γῆς
ποίμναις ὁμαρτεῖ πόλεος ἐκβεβλημένος·
κέλευε δ᾽ αὐτὸν τῶνδ᾽ ἐμοῦσαφιγμένων
ἐλθεῖν, ξένων τ᾽ ἐς δαῖτα πορσῦναί τινα.
ἡσθήσεταί τοι καὶ προσεύξεται θεοῖς,   415
ζῶντ᾽ εἰσακούσας παῖδ᾽ ὃν ἐκσῴζει ποτέ.
οὐ γὰρ πατρῴων ἐκ δόμων μητρὸς πάρα
λάβοιμεν ἄν τι· πικρὰ δ᾽ ἀγγείλαιμεν ἄν,
εἰ ζῶντ᾽ Ὀρέστην ἡ τάλαιν᾽ αἴσθοιτ᾽ ἔτι.

38

rather than a man with wealth. I applaud
how this man has received me in his home,
although I could have hoped your brother,
enjoying prosperity, might lead me in
to a successful house. Perhaps he'll come.
The oracles of Loxias are strong.
But I dismiss mere human prophecy.9   [400]

[Pylades, Orestes, and their servants go into the house]

CHORUS LEADER
    Now, Electra, our hearts are warm with joy—
    more than they were before. Your fortunes
    may perhaps advance, although that's difficult,
    and end up standing in a better place.

ELECTRA
    Reckless man, you know how poor your house is—
    why did you offer your hospitality
    to people so much greater than yourself?

PEASANT
    What's wrong? If they're as well bred as they seem,
    won't they be just as happy with small men
    as with the great?

ELECTRA
                 Well, you're one of the small—
    and since you've now committed this mistake,
    go to that dear old servant of my father's.
    He's been expelled from town and tends his flocks
    by the Tanaus river, which cuts a line   [410]
    between lands of Argos and of Sparta.
    Tell him this—now these people have arrived,
    he must come and provide our guests some food.
    He'll be happy to do that and offer
    prayers up to the gods, after he finds out
    the child he rescued once is still alive.
    From my mother and my ancestral home
    we'd get nothing—we'd bring them bitter news
    if that cruel-hearted woman were to learn
    Orestes is still living.

ΑΥΤΟΥΡΓΟΣ

ἀλλ᾽, εἰ δοκεῖ σοι, τούσδ᾽ ἀπαγγελῶ λόγους   420
γέροντι· χώρει δ᾽ ἐς δόμους ὅσον τάχος
καὶ τἄνδον ἐξάρτυε. πολλά τοι γυνὴ
χρῄζουσ᾽ ἂν εὕροι δαιτὶ προσφορήματα.
ἔστιν δὲ δὴ τοσαῦτά γ᾽ ἐν δόμοις ἔτι,
ὥσθ᾽ ἕν γ᾽ ἐπ᾽ ἦμαρ τούσδε πληρῶσαι βορᾶς.   425
ἐν τοῖς τοιούτοις δ᾽ ἡνίκ᾽ ἂν γνώμης πέσω,
σκοπῶ τὰ χρήμαθ᾽ ὡς ἔχει μέγα σθένος,
ξένοις τε δοῦναι σῶμά τ᾽ ἐς νόσους πεσὸν
δαπάναισι σῶσαι· τῆς δ᾽ ἐφ᾽ ἡμέραν βορᾶς
ἐς σμικρὸν ἥκει· πᾶς γὰρ ἐμπλησθεὶς ἀνὴρ   430
ὁ πλούσιός τε χὠ πένης ἴσον φέρει.

ΧΟΡΟΣ

κλεινᾶι νᾶες, αἵ ποτ᾽ ἔβατε Τροίαν
   τοῖς ἀμετρήτοις ἐρετμοῖς
  πέμπουσαι χοροὺς μετὰ Νηρῄδων,
   ἵν᾽ ὁ φίλαυλος ἔπαλλε δελ-   435
   φὶς πρῴραις κυανεμβόλοι-
    σιν εἱλισσόμενος,
   πορεύων τὸν τᾶς Θέτιδος
  κοῦφον ἅλμα ποδῶν Ἀχιλῆ
   σὺν Ἀγαμέμνονι Τρωίας   440
    ἐπὶ Σιμουντίδας ἀκτάς.

Νηρῇδες δ᾽ Εὐβοῖδας ἄκρας λιποῦσαι
  μόχθους ἀσπιστὰς ἀκμόνων
  Ἡφαίστου χρυσέων ἔφερον τευχέων,
  ἀνά τε Πήλιον ἀνά τε πρυ-
  μνὰς Ὄσσας ἱερᾶς νάπας   445
   † Νυμφαίας σκοπιὰς
  κόρας μάτευσ᾽, † ἔνθα πατὴρ
  ἱππότας τρέφεν Ἑλλάδι φῶς
  Θέτιδος εἰνάλιον γόνον
   ταχύπορον πόδ᾽ Ἀτρείδαις.   450

PEASANT

All right then,
I'll take that message to the old man,   [420]
if that's what you think. But you should go
inside the house as soon as possible
to get things ready there. If she want to,
surely a woman can find many things
to make into a meal. Within the house
there's still enough to fill them up with food
for one day at least. It's at times like this
when my thoughts can't sort out how to manage,
I think of the great power money has
for giving things to strangers and paying
to save a body whenever it falls sick.
The food we need each day doesn't come to much,
and, rich or poor, all men eat their fill   [430]
with the same amount of food.

[The Peasant and Electra move into the house, leaving the Chorus alone on stage]

CHORUS

You famous ships which once sailed off to Troy
to the beat of countless oars,
leading the Nereids in their dance,
while the flute-loving dolphin leapt
and rolled around your dark-nosed prows,
conveying Achilles, Thetis's son,
whose feet had such a nimble spring,
and Agamemnon, too, off to Troy,   [440]
to the river banks of the Simois.[10]

Leaving Euboea's headland points,
Nereids carried from Hephaestus' forge
his labours on the golden shield and armour,
up to Pelion, along the wooded slopes
of sacred Ossa, where the nymphs keep watch,
and searched those maidens out,
in places the old horseman trained
sea-dwelling Thetis' son   [450]
to be a shining light for Hellas,
swift runner for the sons of Atreus.[11]

Euripides

Ἰλιόθεν δ' ἔκλυόν τινος ἐν λιμέσιν
   Ναυπλίοισι βεβῶτος
    τᾶς σᾶς, ὦ Θέτιδος παῖ,
κλεινᾶς ἀσπίδος ἐν κύκλῳ
τοιάδε σήματα, δείματα   455
   Φρύγια, τετύχθαι·
περιδρόμῳ μὲν ἴτυος ἕδρᾳ
Περσέα λαιμοτόμαν ὑπὲρ
   ἁλὸς ποτανοῖσι πεδί-
λοισι φυὰν Γοργόνος ἴ-   460
σχειν, Διὸς ἀγγέλῳ σὺν Ἑρ-
   μᾷ, τῷ Μαί-
   ας ἀγροτῆρι κούρῳ·   463

ἐν δὲ μέσῳ κατέλαμπε σάκει φαέθων
   κύκλος ἀελίοιο
   ἵπποις ἄμ πτεροέσσαις   465
ἄστρων τ' αἰθέριοι χοροί,
Πλειάδες, Ὑάδες, Ἕκτορος
   ὄμμασι τροπαῖοι·
ἐπὶ δὲ χρυσοτύπῳ κράνει
Σφίγγες ὄνυξιν ἀοίδιμον   470
   ἄγραν φέρουσαι· περιπλεύ-
ρῳ δὲ κύτει πύρπνοος ἔ-
σπευδε δρόμῳ λέαινα χαλ-
   αῖς Πειρη-
   ναῖον ὁρῶσα πῶλον.   475

ἄορι δ' ἐν φονίῳ τετραβάμονες ἵπποι ἔπαλ-
   λον, κελαινὰ δ' ἀμφὶ νῶθ' ἵετο κόνις.
   τοιῶνδ' ἄνακτα δοριπόνων   479
ἔκανεν ἀνδρῶν, Τυνδαρίς,
σὰ λέχεα, κακόφρων κούρα.
τοιγάρ σέ ποτ' οὐρανίδαι   483
πέμψουσιν θανάτοις· ἦ σὰν
ἔτ' ἔτι φόνιον ὑπὸ δέραν   485
ὄψομαι αἷμα χυθὲν σιδάρῳ.

42

I heard from a man who'd come from Troy
and reached the harbour in Nauplia
that on the circle of your splendid shield,
O son of Thetis, were these images,
a terror to the Phyrgians—
on the rim around the edge
was Perseus in his flying sandals   [460]
holding up above the sea
the Gorgon's head and severed throat,
accompanied by Zeus' messenger
Hermes, Maia's country child.[12]

In the centre of the shield
the circle of the sun shone out
with his team of winged horses.
In the heavens stars were dancing,
the Pleides and Hyades,
a dreadful sight for Hector's eyes.
On his helmet made of hammered gold   [470]
in their talons sphinxes clutched
their prey seduced by song.
And on the breastplate breathing fire
a lioness with claws raced at top speed
eying a young horse of Pirene.[13]

And on his murderous sword
four horses galloped—above their backs
clouds of black dust billowed.
Evil-minded daughter of Tyndareus,   [480]
your bed mate killed the king
of spear-bearing warriors like these.
And for that death the heavenly gods
will one day pay you back with death.
Yes, one day I will see your blood,
a lethal flow beneath your throat,
sliced through with sword of iron.

Euripides

ΠΡΕΣΒΥΣ
ποῦ ποῦ νεᾶνις πότνι᾽ ἐμὴ δέσποινά τε,
Ἀγαμέμνονος παῖς, ὅν ποτ᾽ ἐξέθρεψ᾽ ἐγώ;
ὡς πρόσβασιν τῶνδ᾽ ὀρθίαν οἴκων ἔχει
ῥυσῷ γέροντι τῷδε προσβῆναι ποδί.   490
ὅμως δὲ πρός γε τοὺς φίλους ἐξελκτέον
διπλῆν ἄκανθαν καὶ παλίρροπον γόνυ.
ὦ θύγατερ—ἄρτι γάρ σε πρὸς δόμοις ὁρῶ—
ἥκω φέρων σοι τῶν ἐμῶν βοσκημάτων
ποίμνης νεογνὸν θρέμμ᾽ ὑποσπάσας τόδε   495
στεφάνους τε τευχέων τ᾽ ἐξελὼν τυρεύματα,
παλαιόν τε θησαύρισμα Διονύσου τόδε
ὀσμῇ κατῆρες, μικρόν, ἀλλ᾽ ἐπεσβαλεῖν
ἡδὺ σκύφον τοῦδ᾽ ἀσθενεστέρῳ ποτῷ.
ἴτω φέρων τις τοῖς ξένοις τάδ᾽ ἐς δόμους·   500
ἐγὼ δὲ τρύχει τῷδ᾽ ἐμῶν πέπλων κόρας
δακρύοισι τέγξας ἐξομόρξασθαι θέλω.

ΗΛΕΚΤΡΑ
τί δ᾽, ὦ γεραιέ, διάβροχον τόδ᾽ ὄμμ᾽ ἔχεις;
μῶν τἀμὰ διὰ χρόνου σ᾽ ἀνέμνησεν κακά;
ἢ τὰς Ὀρέστου τλήμονας φυγὰς στένεις   505
καὶ πατέρα τὸν ἐμόν, ὅν ποτ᾽ ἐν χεροῖν ἔχων
ἀνόνητ᾽ ἔθρεψας σοί τε καὶ τοῖς σοῖς φίλοις;

ΠΡΕΣΒΥΣ
ἀνόνηθ᾽· ὅμως δ᾽ οὖν τοῦτό γ᾽ οὐκ ἠνεσχόμην.
ἦλθον γὰρ αὐτοῦ πρὸς τάφον πάρεργ᾽ ὁδοῦ
καὶ προσπεσὼν ἔκλαυσ᾽ ἐρημίας τυχών,   510
σπονδάς τε, λύσας ἀσκὸν ὃν φέρω ξένοις,
ἔσπεισα, τύμβῳ δ᾽ ἀμφέθηκα μυρσίνας.
πυρᾶς δ᾽ ἐπ᾽ αὐτῆς οἶν μελάγχιμον πόκῳ
σφάγιον ἐσεῖδον αἷμά τ᾽ οὐ πάλαι χυθὲν
ξανθῆς τε χαίτης βοστρύχους κεκαρμένους.   515

44

[Enter the Old Man. Electra comes out of the house during his speech]

OLD MAN

So where is she? Where is my young lady,
my mistress — the child of Agamemnon,
whom I once raised? How steep this path is
up to her place for a withered old man   [490]
going uphill on foot! Still, they are my friends,
so I must drag my doubled-over spine
and tottering legs up here. O my daughter —
now I can see you there before the house —
I've come bringing here from my own livestock
this newborn lamb taken from its mother,
garlands, cheeses I got from the barrel,
and this ancient treasure from Dionysus —
it smells so rich! There's not much of it,
but still it's sweet to add a tankard of it
to a weaker drink. Go now. Let someone
take these things for guests inside the house.   [500]
I want to use a rag, a piece of clothing,
to wipe my eyes. I've drenched them with weeping.

ELECTRA

Why are your eyes so soaking wet, old man?
I'm not reminding you about our troubles
after all this time? Or are you moaning
about Orestes in his wretched exile
and about my father, whom you once held
in your arms and raised, though your friends and you
derived no benefits from it?

OLD MAN

                                    That's right —
it didn't help us. But still, there's one thing
I could not endure. So I went to his tomb,
a detour on the road. I was alone,   [510]
so I fell down and wept, then opened up
the bag of wine I'm bringing for the guests,
poured a libation, and spread out there
some myrtle sprigs around the monument.
But then I saw an offering on the altar,
a black-fleeced sheep — there was blood as well,
shed not long before, and some sliced off curls,

45

κἀθαύμασ᾽, ὦ παῖ, τίς ποτ᾽ ἀνθρώπων ἔτλη
πρὸς τύμβον ἐλθεῖν· οὐ γὰρ Ἀργείων γέ τις.
ἀλλ᾽ ἦλθ᾽ ἴσως που σὸς κασίγνητος λάθρᾳ,
μολὼν δ᾽ ἐθαύμασ᾽ ἄθλιον τύμβον πατρός.
σκέψαι δὲ χαίτην προστιθεῖσα σῇ κόμῃ,   520
εἰ χρῶμα ταὐτὸν κουρίμης ἔσται τριχός·
φιλεῖ γάρ, αἷμα ταὐτὸν οἷς ἂν ᾖ πατρός,
τὰ πόλλ᾽ ὅμοια σώματος πεφυκέναι.

ΗΛΕΚΤΡΑ

οὐκ ἄξι᾽ ἀνδρός, ὦ γέρον, σοφοῦ λέγεις,
εἰ κρυπτὸν ἐς γῆν τήνδ᾽ ἂν Αἰγίσθου φόβῳ   525
δοκεῖς ἀδελφὸν τὸν ἐμὸν εὐθαρσῆ μολεῖν.
ἔπειτα χαίτης πῶς συνοίσεται πλόκος,
ὁ μὲν παλαίστραις ἀνδρὸς εὐγενοῦς τραφείς,
ὁ δὲ κτενισμοῖς θῆλυς; ἀλλ᾽ ἀμήχανον.
πολλοῖς δ᾽ ἂν εὕροις βοστρύχους ὁμοπτέρους   530
καὶ μὴ γεγῶσιν αἵματος ταὐτοῦ, γέρον.

ΠΡΕΣΒΥΣ

σὺ δ᾽ εἰς ἴχνος βᾶσ᾽ ἀρβύλης σκέψαι βάσιν
εἰ σύμμετρος σῷ ποδὶ γενήσεται, τέκνον.

ΗΛΕΚΤΡΑ

πῶς δ᾽ ἂν γένοιτ᾽ ἂν ἐν κραταιλέῳ πέδῳ
γαίας ποδῶν ἔκμακτρον; εἰ δ᾽ ἔστιν τόδε,   535
δυοῖν ἀδελφοῖν ποὺς ἂν οὐ γένοιτ᾽ ἴσος
ἀνδρός τε καὶ γυναικός, ἀλλ᾽ ἄρσην κρατεῖ.

ΠΡΕΣΒΥΣ

οὐκ ἔστιν, εἰ καὶ γῆν κασίγνητος μολών.

.   .   .   .

κερκίδος ὅτῳ γνοίης ἂν ἐξύφασμα σῆς,   538
ἐν ᾧ ποτ᾽ αὐτὸν ἐξέκλεψα μὴ θανεῖν;

46

locks of yellow hair. My child, I wondered
what man would ever dare approach that tomb.
It surely wasn't any man from Argos.
Perhaps you brother has come back somehow,
in secret, and as he came, paid tribute
to his father's tomb. You should go inspect   [520]
the lock of hair, set it against your own—
see if the colour of the severed hair
matches yours. Those sharing common blood
from the same father will by nature have
many features which are very similar.

ELECTRA
What you've just said, old man, is not worth much.
You've no sense at all, if you think my brother,
a brave man, would sneak into this country
in secret, because he fears Aegisthus.
And how can two locks of hair look alike,
when one comes from a well-bred man and grew
in wrestling schools, whereas the other one
was shaped by woman's combing? That's useless.
Old man, with many people you could find   [530]
hair which looked alike, although by birth
they're not the same.

OLD MAN
                              Then stand in the footprint,
my child, and see if the impression there
is the same size as your foot.

ELECTRA
                              How could a foot
make any imprint on such stony ground?
And even if it could, a brother's print
would not match his sister's foot in size.
The man's is bigger.

OLD MAN
                              If your brother's come,
isn't there a piece of weaving from your loom
by which you might know his identity?
What about the weaving he was wrapped in
when I rescued him from death?   [540]

ΗΛΕΚΤΡΑ

οὐκ οἶσθ᾽, Ὀρέστης ἡνίκ᾽ ἐκπίπτει χθονός,   540

νέαν μ᾽ ἔτ᾽ οὖσαν; εἰ δὲ κἄκρεκον πέπλους,

πῶς ἂν τότ᾽ ὢν παῖς ταὐτὰ νῦν ἔχοι φάρη,

εἰ μὴ ξυναύξοινθ᾽ οἱ πέπλοι τῷ σώματι;

ἀλλ᾽ ἤ τις αὐτοῦ τάφον ἐποικτίρας ξένος

† ἐκείρατ᾽, ἢ τῆσδε σκοποὺς λαβὼν χθονὸς † . . .   545

ΠΡΕΣΒΥΣ

οἱ δὲ ξένοι ποῦ; βούλομαι γὰρ εἰσιδὼν

αὐτοὺς ἔρεσθαι σοῦ κασιγνήτου πέρι.

ΗΛΕΚΤΡΑ

οἵδ᾽ ἐκ δόμων βαίνουσι λαιψηρῷ ποδί.

ΠΡΕΣΒΥΣ

ἀλλ᾽ εὐγενεῖς μέν, ἐν δὲ κιβδήλῳ τόδε·

πολλοὶ γὰρ ὄντες εὐγενεῖς εἰσιν κακοί.   550

ὅμως δέ.— χαίρειν τοὺς ξένους προσεννέπω.

ΟΡΕΣΤΗΣ

χαῖρ᾽, ὦ γεραιέ.— τοῦ ποτ᾽, Ἠλέκτρα, τόδε

παλαιὸν ἀνδρὸς λείψανον φίλων κυρεῖ;

ΗΛΕΚΤΡΑ

οὗτος τὸν ἀμὸν πατέρ᾽ ἔθρεψεν, ὦ ξένε.

ΟΡΕΣΤΗΣ

τί φῄς; ὅδ᾽ ὃς σὸν ἐξέκλειψε σύγγονον;   555

ΗΛΕΚΤΡΑ

ὅδ᾽ ἔσθ᾽ ὁ σώσας κεῖνον, εἴπερ ἔστ᾽ ἔτι.

ELECTRA

Don't you know
at the time Orestes left this country
I was still young? And if I'd made his clothes
when he was just a child, how could he have
the same ones now, unless the robes he wore
increased in size as his body grew? No.
Either some stranger, pitying the grave,
cut his hair, or someone slipped past the guard.[14]

OLD MAN

Where are your guests? I'd like to see them
and ask about your brother.

[Orestes and Pylades come out of the house]

ELECTRA

Here they are —
coming outside in a hurry.

OLD MAN

They're well born,   [550]
but that may be misleading. Many men
of noble parentage are a bad lot.
But still I'll say welcome to these strangers.

ORESTES

Welcome to you, old man. So, Electra,
this ancient remnant of a man — to whom
among your friends does he belong?

ELECTRA

Stranger,
this man is the one who raised my father.

ORESTES

What are you saying? Is this the man
who stole away your brother?

ELECTRA

He's the one
who rescued him, if he's still alive.

49

ΟΡΕΣΤΗΣ

ἔα·

τί μ᾽ ἐσδέδορκεν ὥσπερ ἀργύρου σκοπῶν

λαμπρὸν χαρακτῆρ᾽; ἢ προσεικάζει μέ τῳ;

ΗΛΕΚΤΡΑ

ἴσως Ὀρέστου σ᾽ ἧλιχ᾽ ἥδεται βλέπων.   560

ΟΡΕΣΤΗΣ

φίλου γε φωτός. τί δὲ κυκλεῖ πέριξ πόδα;

ΗΛΕΚΤΡΑ

καὐτὴ τόδ᾽ εἰσορῶσα θαυμάζω, ξένε.

ΠΡΕΣΒΥΣ

ὦ πότνι᾽, εὔχου, θύγατερ Ἠλέκτρα, θεοῖς.

ΗΛΕΚΤΡΑ

τί τῶν ἀπόντων ἢ τί τῶν ὄντων πέρι;

ΠΡΕΣΒΥΣ

λαβεῖν φίλον θησαυρόν, ὃν φαίνει θεός   565

ΗΛΕΚΤΡΑ

ἰδού· καλῶ θεούς. ἢ τί δὴ λέγεις, γέρον;

ΠΡΕΣΒΥΣ

βλέψον νυν ἐς τόνδ᾽, ὦ τέκνον, τὸν φίλτατον.

ΗΛΕΚΤΡΑ

πάλαι δέδορκα, μὴ σύ γ᾽ οὐκέτ᾽ εὖ φρονῇς.

ΠΡΕΣΒΥΣ

οὐκ εὖ φρονῶ ᾽γὼ σὸν κασίγνητον βλέπων;

ΗΛΕΚΤΡΑ

πῶς εἶπας, ὦ γεραί᾽, ἀνέλπιστον λόγον;   570

50

ORESTES

Wait!
Why's he inspecting me, as if checking
some clear mark stamped on a piece of silver?
Is he comparing me with someone?

ELECTRA

It could be he's happy looking at you   [560]
as someone who's a comrade of Orestes.

ORESTES

Well, yes, Orestes is a friend of mine,
but why's he going in circles round me?

ELECTRA

Stranger, as I watch him, I'm surprised as well.

OLD MAN

O my daughter Electra, my lady—
pray to the gods.

ELECTRA

What should I pray for,
something here or something far away?

OLD MAN

To get yourself a treasure which you love,
something the god is making manifest.

ELECTRA

Watch this then. I'm summoning the gods.
Is that what you mean, old man?

OLD MAN

Now, my child,
look at this man, the one you love the most.

ELECTRA

I've been observing for a long time now
to see if your mind is working as it should.

OLD MAN

I'm not thinking straight if I see your brother?

ELECTRA

What are you talking about, old man,   [570]
making such an unexpected claim?

ΠΡΕΣΒΥΣ

ὁρᾶν Ὀρέστην τόνδε τὸν Ἀγαμέμνονος.

ΗΛΕΚΤΡΑ

ποῖον χαρακτῆρ᾽ εἰσιδών, ᾧ πείσομαι;

ΠΡΕΣΒΥΣ

οὐλὴν παρ᾽ ὀφρύν, ἥν ποτ᾽ ἐν πατρὸς δόμοις
νεβρὸν διώκων σοῦ μέθ᾽ ἡμάχθη πεσών.

ΗΛΕΚΤΡΑ

πῶς φῄς; ὁρῶ μὲν πτώματος τεκμήριον.   575

ΠΡΕΣΒΥΣ

ἔπειτα μέλλεις προσπίτνειν τοῖς φιλτάτοις;

ΗΛΕΚΤΡΑ

ἀλλ᾽ οὐκέτ᾽, ὦ γεραιέ· συμβόλοισι γὰρ
τοῖς σοῖς πέπεισμαι θυμόν.—ὦ χρόνῳ φανείς,
ἔχω σ᾽ ἀέλπτως . . .

ΟΡΕΣΤΗΣ

                    κἀξ ἐμοῦ γ᾽ ἔχῃ χρόνῳ.

ΗΛΕΚΤΡΑ

οὐδέποτε δόξασα.

ΟΡΕΣΤΗΣ

                    οὐδ᾽ ἐγὼ γὰρ ἤλπισα.   580

ΗΛΕΚΤΡΑ

ἐκεῖνος εἶ σύ;

ΟΡΕΣΤΗΣ

                    σύμμαχός γέ σοι μόνος.
ἢν δ᾽ ἀνσπάσωμαί γ᾽ ὃν μετέρχομαι βόλον . . .
πέποιθα δ᾽· ἢ χρὴ μηκέθ᾽ ἡγεῖσθαι θεούς,
εἰ τἄδικ᾽ ἔσται τῆς δίκης ὑπέρτερα.

OLD MAN

    I'm looking at Orestes, Agamemnon's son.

ELECTRA

    What mark do you see which will convince me?

OLD MAN

    A scar along his eyebrow. He fell one day
    and drew blood. He was in his father's house
    chasing down a fawn with you.

ELECTRA

                  What are you saying?
    I do see the mark of that fall. . . .

OLD MAN

                     Then why delay
    embracing the one you love the most?

ELECTRA

    No. I'll no longer hesitate — my heart
    has been won over by that sign of yours.

[Electra moves over to Orestes and they embrace]

ELECTRA

    You've appeared at last. I'm holding you . . .
    beyond my hopes.

ORESTES

                 After all this time,
    I'm embracing you.

ELECTRA

              I never expected this.   [580]

ORESTES

    This was something I, too, could not hope for.

ELECTRA

    Are you really him?

ORESTES

                Yes. Your sole ally.
    If in my net I can catch the prey I'm after . . .
    But I'm confident. For if wrongful acts
    overpower justice, then no longer
    should we put any faith in gods.

ΧΟΡΟΣ

ἔμολες ἔμολες, ὤ, χρόνιος ἁμέρα,   585
κατέλαμψας, ἔδειξας ἐμφανῆ
πόλει πυρσόν, ὃς παλαιᾷ φυγᾷ
πατρίων ἀπὸ δωμάτων τάλας
ἀλαίνων ἔβα.
θεὸς αὖ θεὸς ἁμετέραν τις ἄγει   590
νίκαν, ὦ φίλα.
ἄνεχε χέρας, ἄνεχε λόγον, ἵει λιτὰς
ἐς θεούς, τύχᾳ σοι τύχᾳ
κασίγνητον ἐμβατεῦσαι πόλιν.   595

ΟΡΕΣΤΗΣ

εἰέν· φίλας μὲν ἡδονὰς ἀσπασμάτων
ἔχω, χρόνῳ δὲ καὖθις αὐτὰ δώσομεν.
σὺ δ᾽, ὦ γεραιέ—καίριος γὰρ ἦλυθες—
λέξον, τί δρῶν ἂν φονέα τεισαίμην πατρός;
[μητέρα τε κοινωνὸν ἀνοσίων γάμων;]   600
ἔστιν τί μοι κατ᾽ Ἄργος εὐμενὲς φίλων;
ἢ πάντ᾽ ἀνεσκευάσμεθ᾽, ὥσπερ αἱ τύχαι;
τῷ ξυγγένωμαι; νύχιος ἢ καθ᾽ ἡμέραν;
ποίαν ὁδὸν τραπώμεθ᾽ εἰς ἐχθροὺς ἐμούς;

ΠΡΕΣΒΥΣ

ὦ τέκνον, οὐδεὶς δυστυχοῦντί σοι φίλος.   605
εὕρημα γάρ τοι χρῆμα γίγνεται τόδε,
κοινῇ μετασχεῖν τἀγαθοῦ καὶ τοῦ κακοῦ.
σὺ δ᾽—ἐκ βάθρων γὰρ πᾶς ἀνήρησαι φίλοις
οὐδ᾽ ἐλλέλοιπας ἐλπίδ᾽—ἴσθι μου κλύων,
ἐν χειρὶ τῇ σῇ πάντ᾽ ἔχεις καὶ τῇ τύχῃ,   610
πατρῷον οἶκον καὶ πόλιν λαβεῖν σέθεν.

ΟΡΕΣΤΗΣ

τί δῆτα δρῶντες τοῦδ᾽ ἂν ἐξικοίμεθα;

ΠΡΕΣΒΥΣ

κτανὼν Θυέστου παῖδα σήν τε μητέρα.

54

CHORUS

    You've come, ah, you've come,
    this day we've waited for so long.
    You've shone out and lit a beacon
    for the city, the man who long ago
    went out in exile from his father's house
    to roam around in misery.
    Now a god, my friend, some god   [590]
    brings victory. Lift up your hands,
    lift up your words, send prayers
    up to the gods for your success,
    good fortune for your brother
    as he goes in the city.

ORESTES

    Well, I've had the loving joys of welcome.
    In time I'll give them back to you again.
    You, old man, you've come at a good time.
    Tell me this—what should I do to repay
    my father's murderer and my mother,
    his partner in this sacrilegious marriage?   [600]
    Do I have any friends who'll help in Argos?
    Or are they all gone, just like my fortune?
    Who can I make my ally? Do we meet
    during the day or at night? What pathway
    do I turn towards to fight my enemies?

OLD MAN

    My child, in your bad times you've got no friends.
    It's a great benefit to find someone
    who'll share with you the good times and the bad.
    But since, as far as your friends can see,
    you and the foundations of your house
    have been wiped out completely and you've left
    no hope for them, then pay attention to me.
    Know this—the only things which you possess   [610]
    to win back your father's home and city
    are your own hands and your good fortune.

ORESTES

    What then should I do to succeed in this?

OLD MAN

    Kill Thyestes' son and your own mother.[15]

ΟΡΕΣΤΗΣ

ἥκω 'πὶ τόνδε στέφανον· ἀλλὰ πῶς λάβω;

ΠΡΕΣΒΥΣ

τειχέων μὲν ἐλθὼν ἐντὸς οὐδ' ἂν εἰ θέλοις.　　615

ΟΡΕΣΤΗΣ

φρουραῖς κέκασται δεξιαῖς τε δορυφόρων;

ΠΡΕΣΒΥΣ

ἔγνως· φοβεῖται γάρ σε κοὐχ εὕδει σαφῶς.

ΟΡΕΣΤΗΣ

εἶέν· σὺ δὴ τοὐνθένδε βούλευσον, γέρον.

ΠΡΕΣΒΥΣ

κἀμοῦ γ' ἄκουσον· ἄρτι γάρ μ' ἐσῆλθέ τι.

ΟΡΕΣΤΗΣ

ἐσθλόν τι μηνύσειας, αἰσθοίμην δ' ἐγώ.　　620

ΠΡΕΣΒΥΣ

Αἴγισθον εἶδον, ἡνίχ' εἷρπον ἐνθάδε.

ΟΡΕΣΤΗΣ

προσηκάμην τὸ ῥηθέν. ἐν ποίοις τόποις;

ΠΡΕΣΒΥΣ

ἀγρῶν πέλας τῶνδ' ἱπποφορβίων ἔπι.

ΟΡΕΣΤΗΣ

τί δρῶνθ'; ὁρῶ γὰρ ἐλπίδ' ἐξ ἀμηχάνων.

ΠΡΕΣΒΥΣ

Νύμφαις ἐπόρσυν' ἔροτιν, ὡς ἔδοξέ μοι.　　625

56

ORESTES

That's the crown of victory I'm after.
But how do I get my hands on it?

OLD MAN

Well, even if you want to try it,
don't go inside the walls.

ORESTES

Is he well supplied
with garrison troops and bodyguards?

OLD MAN

Yes, he is.
He's afraid of you and does not sleep well.

ORESTES

Well, old man, you must give me some advice
about what happens next.

OLD MAN

Then listen to me.
A thought has just occurred to me.

ORESTES

I hope you come up with something good   [620]
which I can understand.

OLD MAN

While coming here,
I saw Aegisthus.

ORESTES

I'll accept those words.
Where was he?[16]

OLD MAN

In the fields close to his stables.

ORESTES

What was he doing? I can see some hope
emerging from our desperate circumstances.

OLD MAN

He was setting up a banquet for the Nymphs —
that's what it seemed to me.

Euripides

ΟΡΕΣΤΗΣ

τροφεῖα παίδων ἢ πρὸ μέλλοντος τόκου;

ΠΡΕΣΒΥΣ

οὐκ οἶδα πλὴν ἕν· βουσφαγεῖν ὡπλίζετο.

ΟΡΕΣΤΗΣ

πόσων μετ᾽ ἀνδρῶν; ἢ μόνος δμώων μέτα;

ΠΡΕΣΒΥΣ

οὐδεὶς παρῆν Ἀργεῖος, οἰκεία δὲ χείρ.

ΟΡΕΣΤΗΣ

οὔ πού τις ὅστις γνωριεῖ μ᾽ ἰδών, γέρον;   630

ΠΡΕΣΒΥΣ

δμῶες μέν εἰσιν, οἳ σέ γ᾽ οὐκ εἶδόν ποτε.

ΟΡΕΣΤΗΣ

ἡμῖν ἂν εἶεν, εἰ κρατοῖμεν, εὐμενεῖς;

ΠΡΕΣΒΥΣ

δούλων γὰρ ἴδιον τοῦτο, σοὶ δὲ σύμφορον.

ΟΡΕΣΤΗΣ

πῶς οὖν ἂν αὐτῷ πλησιασθείην ποτέ;

ΠΡΕΣΒΥΣ

στείχων ὅθεν σε βουθυτῶν ἐσόψεται.   635

ΟΡΕΣΤΗΣ

ὁδὸν παρ᾽ αὐτήν, ὡς ἔοικ᾽, ἀγροὺς ἔχει;

ΠΡΕΣΒΥΣ

ὅθεν γ᾽ ἰδών σε δαιτὶ κοινωνὸν καλεῖ.

ΟΡΕΣΤΗΣ

πικρόν γε συνθοινάτορ᾽, ἢν θεὸς θέλῃ.

58

ORESTES

But was it for
a child that's now being raised or some new birth?[17]

OLD MAN

I only know one thing—there was an ox.
He was preparing it for sacrifice.

ORESTES

How many men did he have there with him?
Or was he by himself with his attendants?

OLD MAN

No Argives, only a group of servants.

ORESTES

Old man, there isn't anybody there   [630]
who'll know me if he sees me, is there?

OLD MAN

They're slaves who have never set eyes on you.

ORESTES

If we prevail, will they be on our side?

OLD MAN

Yes. That's what slaves are like. You're lucky.

ORESTES

How do I get close to him?

OLD MAN

You should walk
where he can see you as he sacrifices.

ORESTES

So apparently his fields are by the road?

OLD MAN

Yes. When he catches sight of you from there,
he'll summon you to join the feast.

ORESTES

With god's will,
I'll make a bitter fellow banqueter.

Euripides

ΠΡΕΣΒΥΣ
τοὐνθένδε πρὸς τὸ πῖπτον αὐτὸς ἐννόει.

ΟΡΕΣΤΗΣ
καλῶς ἔλεξας. —ἡ τεκοῦσα δ᾽ ἐστὶ ποῦ;   640

ΠΡΕΣΒΥΣ
Ἄργει· παρέσται δ᾽ οὖν πόσει θοίνην ἔπι.

ΟΡΕΣΤΗΣ
τί δ᾽ οὐχ ἅμ᾽ ἐξωρμᾶτ᾽ ἐμὴ μήτηρ πόσει;

ΠΡΕΣΒΥΣ
ψόγον τρέμουσα δημοτῶν ἐλείπετο.

ΟΡΕΣΤΗΣ
ξυνῆχ᾽· ὕποπτος οὖσα γιγνώσκει πόλει.

ΠΡΕΣΒΥΣ
τοιαῦτα· μισεῖται γὰρ ἀνόσιος γυνή.   645

ΟΡΕΣΤΗΣ
πῶς οὖν ἐκείνην τόνδε τ᾽ ἐν ταὐτῷ κτενῶ;

ΗΛΕΚΤΡΑ
ἐγὼ φόνον γε μητρὸς ἐξαρτύσομαι.

ΟΡΕΣΤΗΣ
καὶ μὴν ἐκεῖνά γ᾽ ἡ τύχη θήσει καλῶς.

ΗΛΕΚΤΡΑ
ὑπηρετείτω μὲν δυοῖν ὄντοιν ὅδε.

ΠΡΕΣΒΥΣ
ἔσται τάδ᾽· εὑρίσκεις δὲ μητρὶ πῶς φόνον;   650

ΗΛΕΚΤΡΑ
λέγ᾽, ὦ γεραιέ, τάδε Κλυταιμήστρᾳ μολών·
λεχώ μ᾽ ἀπάγγελλ᾽ οὖσαν ἄρσενος τόκῳ.

OLD MAN

    From there on you must sort things out yourself,
    whatever happens.

ORESTES

               A shrewd observation.
    What about my mother? Where is she?   [640]

OLD MAN

    In Argos. She'll join her husband at the feast.

ORESTES

    Why did my mother not leave with her husband?

OLD MAN

    She stayed behind because she was afraid
    the citizens would criticize her.

ORESTES

                    I see.
    She knows the city is suspicious of her.

OLD MAN

    That's right. People hate a profane woman.

ORESTES

    How do I kill them both at the same time?

ELECTRA

    I'll set up mother's murder on my own.

ORESTES

    Good fortune will bring us success in this.

ELECTRA

    Let the old man give both of us some help.

ORESTES

    All right. But how will you devise a way   [650]
    to kill our mother?

ELECTRA

              Old man, you must go
    and report this news to Clytaemnestra—
    say I have given birth, and to a son.

61

ΠΡΕΣΒΥΣ

πότερα πάλαι τεκοῦσαν ἢ νεωστὶ δή;

ΗΛΕΚΤΡΑ

δέχ᾽ ἡλίους, ἐν οἷσιν ἁγνεύει λεχώ.

ΠΡΕΣΒΥΣ

καὶ δὴ τί τοῦτο μητρὶ προσβάλλει φόνον;   655

ΗΛΕΚΤΡΑ

ἥξει κλύουσα λόχιά μου νοσήματα.

ΠΡΕΣΒΥΣ

πόθεν; τί δ᾽ αὐτῇ σοῦ μέλειν δοκεῖς, τέκνον;

ΗΛΕΚΤΡΑ

ναί· καὶ δακρύσει γ᾽ ἀξίωμ᾽ ἐμῶν τόκων.

ΠΡΕΣΒΥΣ

ἴσως· πάλιν τοι μῦθον ἐς καμπὴν ἄγε.

ΗΛΕΚΤΡΑ

ἐλθοῦσα μέντοι δῆλον ὡς ἀπόλλυται.   660

ΠΡΕΣΒΥΣ

καὶ μὴν ἐπ᾽ αὐτάς γ᾽ εἶσι σῶν δόμων πύλας.

ΗΛΕΚΤΡΑ

οὐκοῦν τραπέσθαι σμικρὸν εἰς Ἅιδου τόδε;

ΠΡΕΣΒΥΣ

εἰ γὰρ θάνοιμι τοῦτ᾽ ἰδὼν ἐγώ ποτε.

ΗΛΕΚΤΡΑ

πρώτιστα μέν νυν τῷδ᾽ ὑφήγησαι, γέρον . . .

ΠΡΕΣΒΥΣ

Αἴγισθος ἔνθα νῦν θυηπολεῖ θεοῖς;   665

OLD MAN

Born some time ago or quite recently?

ELECTRA

Before my quarantine, ten days ago.[18]

OLD MAN

How does this advance your mother's murder?

ELECTRA

When she learns I've been through birthing pains,
she'll come here.

OLD MAN

                Why would she do that? My child,
do you think she cares for you?

ELECTRA

                        Yes. And she'll weep
because my child is born so common.

OLD MAN

                                Perhaps.
But come back to the point of what you're saying.

ELECTRA

If she comes, then clearly she'll be killed.   [660]

OLD MAN

Well, she'll come to your house, right to the door.

ELECTRA

So it won't take much for her to turn aside
and go to Hades, will it?

OLD MAN

                    Once I see that,
then let me die!

ELECTRA

                But first of all, old man,
you must lead my brother . . . .

OLD MAN

                  To where Aegisthus
is now offering gods his sacrifice.

ΗΛΕΚΤΡΑ

ἔπειτ᾽ ἀπαντῶν μητρὶ τἀπ᾽ ἐμοῦ φράσον.

ΠΡΕΣΒΥΣ

ὥστ᾽ αὐτά γ᾽ ἐκ σοῦ στόματος εἰρῆσθαι δοκεῖν.

ΗΛΕΚΤΡΑ

σὸν ἔργον ἤδη· πρόσθεν εἴληχας φόνου.

ΟΡΕΣΤΗΣ

στείχοιμ᾽ ἄν, εἴ τις ἡγεμὼν γίγνοιθ᾽ ὁδοῦ.

ΠΡΕΣΒΥΣ

καὶ μὴν ἐγὼ πέμποιμ᾽ ἂν οὐκ ἀκουσίως.   670

ΟΡΕΣΤΗΣ

ὦ Ζεῦ Πατρῷε, καὶ Τροπαῖ᾽ ἐχθρῶν γενοῦ . . .

ΗΛΕΚΤΡΑ

οἴκτιρέ θ᾽ ἡμᾶς· οἰκτρὰ γὰρ πεπόνθαμεν . . .

ΠΡΕΣΒΥΣ

οἴκτιρε δῆτα σούς γε φύντας ἐκγόνους.

ΗΛΕΚΤΡΑ

Ἥρα τε, βωμῶν ἢ Μυκηναίων κρατεῖς . . .

ΟΡΕΣΤΗΣ

νίκην δὸς ἡμῖν, εἰ δίκαι᾽ αἰτούμεθα.   675

ΠΡΕΣΒΥΣ

δὸς δῆτα πατρὸς τοῖσδε τιμωρὸν δίκην.

ΟΡΕΣΤΗΣ

σύ τ᾽, ὦ κάτω γῆς ἀνοσίως οἰκῶν πάτερ . . .

ΗΛΕΚΤΡΑ

καὶ Γαῖ᾽ ἄνασσα, χεῖρας ᾗ δίδωμ᾽ ἐμὰς . . .

ΠΡΕΣΒΥΣ

ἄμυν᾽ ἄμυνε τοῖσδε φιλτάτοις τέκνοις.

ELECTRA
. . . then go to my mother. Tell her my news.

OLD MAN
I'll do it so the very words will seem
as if they came from your own mouth.

ELECTRA *[to Orestes]*
Now it's up to you. You've drawn first lot
in this murder sweepstakes.

ORESTES
     Then I'll be off,
if someone will lead me to the road.

OLD MAN
I'm quite willing to take you there myself.   [670]

ORESTES
O Father Zeus, scatter my enemies . . . .

ELECTRA
Pity us—we've suffered pitifully.

OLD MAN
Yes, have pity on them, your descendants.

ELECTRA
And Hera, who rules Mycenae's altars . . .

ORESTES
Give us victory, if what we seek is just.

OLD MAN
Yes, give them justice to avenge their father.

ORESTES
You, too, father, living beneath the earth
through an unholy slaughter.

ELECTRA
     And lady Earth,
whom I strike with my hands.

OLD MAN
     Defend these two.
Defend these children whom you love the most.

ΟΡΕΣΤΗΣ

νῦν πάντα νεκρὸν ἐλθὲ σύμμαχον λαβών.　　680

ΗΛΕΚΤΡΑ

οἵπερ γε σὺν σοὶ Φρύγας ἀνήλωσαν δορὶ . . .

ΠΡΕΣΒΥΣ

χῶσοι στυγοῦσιν ἀνοσίους μιάστορας.　　683

ΗΛΕΚΤΡΑ

ἤκουσας, ὦ δείν' ἐξ ἐμῆς μητρὸς παθών;　　682

ΠΡΕΣΒΥΣ

πάντ', οἶδ', ἀκούει τάδε πατήρ· στείχειν δ' ἀκμή.

ΗΛΕΚΤΡΑ

καί σοι προφωνῶ πρὸς τάδ' Αἴγισθον θανεῖν·　　685
ὡς εἰ παλαισθεὶς πτῶμα θανάσιμον πεσῇ,
τέθνηκα κἀγώ, μηδέ με ζῶσαν λέγε·
παίσω γὰρ ἧπαρ τοὐμὸν ἀμφήκει ξίφει.
δόμων ἔσω βᾶσ' εὐτρεπὲς ποήσομαι.
ὡς ἢν μὲν ἔλθῃ πύστις εὐτυχὴς σέθεν,　　690
ὀλολύξεται πᾶν δῶμα· θνῄσκοντος δέ σου
τἀναντί' ἔσται τῶνδε· ταῦτά σοι λέγω.

ΟΡΕΣΤΗΣ

πάντ' οἶδα.

ΗΛΕΚΤΡΑ

　　　　πρὸς τάδ' ἄνδρα γίγνεσθαί σε χρή.
ὑμεῖς δέ μοι, γυναῖκες, εὖ πυρσεύετε
κραυγὴν ἀγῶνος τοῦδε· φρουρήσω δ' ἐγὼ　　695
πρόχειρον ἔγχος χειρὶ βαστάζουσ' ἐμῇ.
οὐ γάρ ποτ' ἐχθροῖς τοῖς ἐμοῖς νικωμένη
δίκην ὑφέξω, σῶμ' ἐμὸν καθυβρίσαι.

ORESTES
Come now, with all the dead as allies.

ELECTRA
Those who in that war and by your side
destroyed the Phrygians.

OLD MAN
           And all those
who hate the sacrilegious and profane.

ELECTRA
Are you listening, those of you who suffered
such terrors at the hand of my own mother?

OLD MAN
Your father hears it all, I know. Time to go.

ELECTRA [*to Orestes*]
He knows everything. You must be a man.[19]
And I'll tell you this—Aegisthus has to die.
If in the struggle with him you fall dead,
then I die as well. Do not think of me
as still alive. I'll take my two-edged sword
and slice into my heart. I'll go inside
and get things ready. If you send good news
the whole house will ring with cries of triumph.
But if you die, things will be different.
These are my words to you.

ORESTES
           I understand.

[*Orestes, Pylades, the Old Man, and the attendants leave. Electra turns to face the Chorus*]

ELECTRA
           And you women,
give a good shout to signal this encounter.
I'll be ready waiting, gripping a sword.
If I'm defeated, I'll never submit,
surrendering to my enemies the right
to violate my body.

[*Electra goes back into the house*]

ΧΟΡΟΣ

ἀταλᾶς ὑπὸ ματρὸς ⟨ἄρν'⟩
  Ἀργείων
ὀρέων ποτὲ κληδὼν ἐν   700
πολιαῖσι μένει φήμαις
εὐαρμόστοις ἐν καλάμοις
Πᾶνα μοῦσαν ἡδύθροον
πνέοντ', ἀγρῶν ταμίαν,
χρυσέαν καλλιπλόκαμον   705
πορεῦσαι. πετρίνοις δ' ἐπι-
στὰς κᾶρυξ ἰάχει βάθροις·
Ἀγορὰν ἀγοράν, Μυκη-
ναῖοι, στείχετε μακαρίων
ὀψόμενοι τυράννων   710
φάσματα † δείματα. . . . χοροὶ δ' Ἀτρει-
δᾶν † ἐγέραιρον οἴκους·

θυμέλαι δ' ἐπίτναντο χρυ-
  σήλατοι,
σελαγεῖτο δ' ἀν' ἄστυ πῦρ
ἐπιβώμιον Ἀργείων·   715
λωτὸς δὲ φθόγγον κελάδει
κάλλιστον, Μουσᾶν θεράπων·
μολπαὶ δ' ηὔξοντ' ἐραταί,
χρυσέας ἀρνὸς ἐπίλογοι,
Θυέστου· κρυφίαις γὰρ εὐ-
ναῖς πείσας ἄλοχον φίλαν   720
Ἀτρέως, τέρας ἐκκομί-
ζει πρὸς δώματα· νεόμενος δ'
εἰς ἀγόρους αὐτεῖ
τὰν κερόεσσαν ἔχειν χρυσεόμαλ-
λον κατὰ δῶμα ποίμναν.   725

τότε δὴ τότε φαεν-
νὰς ἄστρων μετέβασ' ὁδοὺς
Ζεὺς καὶ φέγγος ἀελίου
λευκόν τε πρόσωπον ἀ-
οῦς, τὰ δ' ἕσπερα νῶτ' ἐλαύ-   730

CHORUS

    Among our ancient stories,
    there remains a tale how Pan,
    keeper of the country side,   [700]
    breathing sweet-toned music
    on his harmonious flute,
    once led a golden lamb
    with the fairest fleece of all
    from its tender mother
    in the hills of Argos.
    Standing on the platform stone
    a herald with a loud voice cried,
    "Assemble now, you Mycenaeans,
    move into assembly, and see there
    the terrifying and marvelous things
    belonging to your blessed kings."   [710]
    So choruses gave out their tributes
    to the House of Atreus.

    Altars of hammered gold were dressed,
    while in the city fires blazed
    with Argive sacrifice — a flute,
    the Muses' servant, piped graceful notes,
    and seductive melodies arose
    in honour of the golden lamb,
    which now belonged to Thyestes.
    He'd secretly talked into bed   [720]
    the well-loved wife of Atreus.
    then carries home the marvellous prize,
    and, going to the assembly, says
    he now possesses in his house
    the horned sheep with its fleece of gold.[20]

    But then, at that very moment,
    Zeus changed the paths
    of all the shining stars,
    the radiant glory of the sun,
    and dawn's bright shining face.   [730]
    Across the western reaches of the sky

Euripides

νει θερμᾷ φλογὶ θεοπύρῳ,
νεφέλαι δ᾽ ἔνυδροι πρὸς ἄρ-
κτον, ξηραί τ᾽ Ἀμμωνίδες ἕ-
δραι φθίνουσ᾽ ἀπειρόδροσοι,
καλλίστων ὄμβρων Διόθεν στερεῖσαι.   735

λέγεται, τὰν δὲ πί-
στιν σμικρὰν παρ᾽ ἔμοιγ᾽ ἔχει,
στρέψαι θερμὰν ἀέλιον
χρυσωπὸν ἕδραν ἀλλά-
ξαντα δυστυχίᾳ βροτεί-   740
ῳ θνατᾶς ἕνεκεν δίκας.
φοβεροὶ δὲ βροτοῖσι μῦ-
θοι κέρδος πρὸς θεῶν θεραπεί-
αν. ὧν οὐ μνασθεῖσα πόσιν
κτείνεις, κλεινῶν συγγενέτειρ᾽ ἀδελφῶν.   745

— ἔα ἔα·
φίλαι, βοῆς ἠκούσατ᾽—ἢ δοκῶ κενὴ
ὑπῆλθέ μ᾽;—ὥστε νερτέρα βροντὴ Διός;
ἰδού, τάδ᾽ οὐκ ἄσημα πνεύματ᾽ αἴρεται·
δέσποιν᾽, ἄμειψον δώματ᾽, Ἠλέκτρα, τάδε.   750

ΗΛΕΚΤΡΑ
φίλαι, τί χρῆμα; πῶς ἀγῶνος ἥκομεν;

ΧΟΡΟΣ
οὐκ οἶδα πλὴν ἕν· φόνιον οἰμωγὴν κλύω.

ΗΛΕΚΤΡΑ
ἤκουσα κἀγώ, τηλόθεν μέν, ἀλλ᾽ ὅμως.

ΧΟΡΟΣ
μακρὰν γὰρ ἕρπει γῆρυς, ἐμφανής γε μήν.

ΗΛΕΚΤΡΑ
Ἀργεῖος ὁ στεναγμός· ἦ φίλων ἐμῶν;   755

70

he drove hot flames from heaven.
Rain clouds moved up to the north,
so Ammon's lands were dry—
all withered up, deprived by Zeus
of his most lovely showers of rain.[21]

People speak about these tales,
but in such things my faith is small—
that the sun's hot throne of gold   [740]
turned round, to punish human beings,
in a cause involving mortal men.
But tales which terrify mankind
are profitable and serve the gods.
When you destroyed your husband
your mind was unconcerned with them,
you sister of such glorious brothers.[22]

CHORUS LEADER
    Wait! Hold on! Did you hear a shout, my friends?
    Or has some vain notion overtaken me,
    like Zeus' rumbling underneath the ground?
    Look, breezes are coming up—that's a sign.
    My lady, come out of the house! Electra!   [750]

[Electra comes out of the house]

ELECTRA
    What is it, my friends? How are we faring
    in the struggle?

CHORUS LEADER
                There's only one thing I know—
    I heard the scream of murder.

ELECTRA
                    I heard it, too.
    It came from far away, but I could hear it.

CHORUS LEADER
    Yes, a long way off, but it was clear.

ELECTRA
    Was it someone from Argos moaning,
    or some of my friends?

71

ΧΟΡΟΣ

οὐκ οἶδα· πᾶν γὰρ μείγνυται μέλος βοῆς.

ΗΛΕΚΤΡΑ

σφαγὴν ἀυτεῖς τήνδε μοι· τί μέλλομεν;

ΧΟΡΟΣ

ἔπισχε, τρανῶς ὡς μάθῃς τύχας σέθεν.

ΗΛΕΚΤΡΑ

οὐκ ἔστι· νικώμεσθα· ποῦ γὰρ ἄγγελοι;

ΧΟΡΟΣ

ἥξουσιν· οὔτοι βασιλέα φαῦλον κτανεῖν.   760

ΑΓΓΕΛΟΣ

ὦ καλλίνικοι παρθένοι Μυκηνίδες,
νικῶντ᾽ Ὀρέστην πᾶσιν ἀγγέλλω φίλοις,
Ἀγαμέμνονος δὲ φονέα κείμενον πέδῳ
Αἴγισθον· ἀλλὰ θεοῖσιν εὔχεσθαι χρεών.

ΗΛΕΚΤΡΑ

τίς δ᾽ εἶ σύ; πῶς μοι πιστὰ σημαίνεις τάδε;   765

ΑΓΓΕΛΟΣ

οὐκ οἶσθ᾽ ἀδελφοῦ μ᾽ εἰσορῶσα πρόσπολον;

ΗΛΕΚΤΡΑ

ὦ φίλτατ᾽, ἔκ τοι δείματος δυσγνωσίαν
εἶχον προσώπου· νῦν δὲ γιγνώσκω σε δή.
τί φῇς; τέθνηκε πατρὸς ἐμοῦ στυγνὸς φονεύς;

ΑΓΓΕΛΟΣ

τέθνηκε· δίς σοι ταῦθ᾽, ἃ γοῦν βούλῃ, λέγω.   770

ΗΛΕΚΤΡΑ

ὦ θεοί, Δίκη τε πάνθ᾽ ὁρῶσ᾽, ἦλθές ποτε.
ποίῳ τρόπῳ δὲ καὶ τίνι ῥυθμῷ φόνου
κτείνει Θυέστου παῖδα; βούλομαι μαθεῖν.

CHORUS LEADER

                             I've no idea.
People are shouting. Things are all confused.

ELECTRA

    What you say means my death. Why do I delay?

CHORUS LEADER

    Hold on until you clearly know your fate.

ELECTRA

    No. We're beaten. Where are the messengers?

CHORUS LEADER

    They'll be here. It's no trivial matter   [760]
to assassinate a king.

[Enter a Messenger on the run]

MESSENGER

    O you victorious daughters of Mycenae,
I can report to all Orestes' friends
that he has triumphed, and now Aegisthus,
Agamemnon's murderer, has fallen.
But we must offer prayers up to the gods.

ELECTRA

    Who are you? How can I trust what you've just said?

MESSENGER

    Don't you know me on sight — your brother's servant.

ELECTRA

    You best of friends! I was too full of fear
to recognize your face. But now I know you.
What are you saying? Has that hateful man,
my father's murderer, been killed?

MESSENGER

                            He's dead.   [770]
I've given you the same report twice now.
Obviously you like the sound of it.

ELECTRA

    O you gods, and all-seeing Justice,
you've come at last. How did Orestes kill
Thyestes' son? What was the murder like?
I want to know.

ΑΓΓΕΛΟΣ
ἐπεὶ μελάθρων τῶνδ' ἀπήραμεν πόδα,
ἐσβάντες ἦμεν δίκροτον εἰς ἁμαξιτὸν   775
ἔνθ' ἦν ὁ κλεινὸς τῶν Μυκηναίων ἄναξ.
κυρεῖ δὲ κήποις ἐν καταρρύτοις βεβώς,
δρέπων τερείνης μυρσίνης κάρα πλόκους·
ἰδών τ' ἀυτεῖ· Χαίρετ', ὦ ξένοι· τίνες
πόθεν πορεύεσθ'; ἔστε τ' ἐκ ποίας χθονός;   780
ὁ δ' εἶπ' Ὀρέστης· Θεσσαλοί· πρὸς δ' Ἀλφεὸν
θύσοντες ἐρχόμεσθ' Ὀλυμπίῳ Διί.
κλύων δὲ ταῦτ' Αἴγισθος ἐννέπει τάδε·
Νῦν μὲν παρ' ἡμῖν χρὴ συνεστίους ἐμοὶ
θοίνης γενέσθαι· τυγχάνω δὲ βουθυτῶν   785
Νύμφαις· ἑῷοι δ' ἐξαναστάντες λέχους
ἐς ταὐτὸν ἥξετ'. ἀλλ' ἴωμεν ἐς δόμους —
καὶ ταῦθ' ἅμ' ἠγόρευε καὶ χερὸς λαβὼν
παρῆγεν ἡμᾶς — οὐδ' ἀπαρνεῖσθαι χρεών·
[ἐπεὶ δ' ἐν οἴκοις ἦμεν, ἐννέπει τάδε·]   790
λούτρ' ὡς τάχιστα τοῖς ξένοις τις αἱρέτω,
ὡς ἀμφὶ βωμὸν στῶσι χερνίβων πέλας.
ἀλλ' εἶπ' Ὀρέστης· Ἀρτίως ἡγνίσμεθα
λουτροῖσι καθαροῖς ποταμῶν ῥείθρων ἄπο.
εἰ δὲ ξένους ἀστοῖσι συνθύειν χρεών,   795
Αἴγισθ', ἕτοιμοι κοὐκ ἀπαρνούμεσθ', ἄναξ.
τοῦτον μὲν οὖν μεθεῖσαν ἐκ μέσου λόγον·
λόγχας δὲ θέντες δεσπότου φρουρήματα
δμῶες πρὸς ἔργον πάντες ἵεσαν χέρας·
οἱ μὲν σφαγεῖον ἔφερον, οἱ δ' ἦρον κανᾶ,   800
ἄλλοι δὲ πῦρ ἀνῆπτον ἀμφί τ' ἐσχάρας
λέβητας ὤρθουν· πᾶσα δ' ἐκτύπει στέγη.
λαβὼν δὲ προχύτας μητρὸς εὐνέτης σέθεν
ἔβαλλε βωμούς, τοιάδ' ἐννέπων ἔπη·
Νύμφαι πετραῖαι, πολλάκις με βουθυτεῖν   805
καὶ τὴν κατ' οἴκους Τυνδαρίδα δάμαρτ' ἐμὴν
πράσσοντας ὡς νῦν, τοὺς δ' ἐμοὺς ἐχθροὺς κακῶς

MESSENGER
                          After we'd left this house,
we walked along the two-tracked wagon path
to where Mycenae's famous king might be.
He happened to be walking in his garden,
a well-watered place, cutting soft myrtle shoots
to place in his own hair. When he saw us,
he called out, "Greetings, strangers. Who are you?   [780]
Where are you from? What country is your home?"
Orestes said, "We are from Thessaly,
on our way to the Alpheus river,
to offer sacrifice to Olympian Zeus."
After hearing that, Aegisthus answered,
"You must be my guests, share this feast with us.
It so happens I'm now offering an ox,
sacrificing to the Nymphs. If you get up
out of bed at dawn, you'll be no worse off.
So come, let's go inside the house." Saying this,
he grabbed our arms and led us off the road,
insisting that we must not turn him down.
Once we were inside the house, he said,   [790]
"Let someone bring in water right away,
so these guests can stand around the altar
by the basin where they purify their hands."
But Orestes said, "We've just cleansed ourselves
in pure water from a flowing river.
If strangers must join with the citizens
in making sacrifice, then, Aegisthus,
we are ready and will not refuse, my lord."
Those were the words they spoke in public.
The slaves guarding my master with their spears
set them aside, and they all lent a hand
to do the work, some bringing in the bowl   [800]
to catch the blood, others fetching baskets,
still others kindling fire and setting basins
around the hearth. The whole house echoed.
Then your mother's consort took barley grain,
sprinkled it across the altar, and said,
"Nymphs of the rocks, may I and my wife,
Tyndareus' daughter, in our home
offer frequent sacrifice, enjoying success,
as we do now, and may my enemies

75

—λέγων Ὀρέστην καὶ σέ. δεσπότης δ' ἐμὸς
τἀναντί' ηὔχετ', οὐ γεγωνίσκων λόγους,
λαβεῖν πατρῷα δώματ'. ἐκ κανοῦ δ' ἑλὼν   810
Αἴγισθος ὀρθὴν σφαγίδα, μοσχείαν τρίχα
τεμὼν ἐφ' ἁγνὸν πῦρ ἔθηκε δεξιᾷ,
κἄσφαξ' ἐπ' ὤμων μόσχον ὡς ἦραν χεροῖν
δμῶες, λέγει δὲ σῷ κασιγνήτῳ τάδε·
Ἐκ τῶν καλῶν κομποῦσι τοῖσι Θεσσαλοῖς   815
εἶναι τόδ', ὅστις ταῦρον ἀρταμεῖ καλῶς
ἵππους τ' ὀχμάζει· λαβὲ σίδηρον, ὦ ξένε,
δεῖξόν τε φήμην ἔτυμον ἀμφὶ Θεσσαλῶν.
ὁ δ' εὐκρότητον Δωρίδ' ἁρπάσας χεροῖν,
ῥίψας ἀπ' ὤμων εὐπρεπῆ πορπάματα,   820
Πυλάδην μὲν εἵλετ' ἐν πόνοις ὑπηρέτην,
δμῶας δ' ἀπωθεῖ· καὶ λαβὼν μόσχου πόδα,
λευκὰς ἐγύμνου σάρκας ἐκτείνων χέρα·
θᾶσσον δὲ βύρσαν ἐξέδειρεν ἢ δρομεὺς
δισσοὺς διαύλους ἵππιος διήνυσε,   825
κἀνεῖτο λαγόνας. ἱερὰ δ' ἐς χεῖρας λαβὼν
Αἴγισθος ἤθρει. καὶ λοβὸς μὲν οὐ προσῆν
σπλάγχνοις, πύλαι δὲ καὶ δοχαὶ χολῆς πέλας
κακὰς ἔφαινον τῷ σκοποῦντι προσβολάς.
χὠ μὲν σκυθράζει, δεσπότης δ' ἀνιστορεῖ·   830
Τί χρῆμ' ἀθυμεῖς;—Ὦ ξέν', ὀρρωδῶ τινα
δόλον θυραῖον. ἔστι δ' ἔχθιστος βροτῶν
Ἀγαμέμνονος παῖς πολέμιός τ' ἐμοῖς δόμοις·
ὁ δ' εἶπε· Φυγάδος δῆτα δειμαίνεις δόλον,
πόλεως ἀνάσσων; οὐχ, ὅπως παστήρια   835
θοινασόμεσθα, Φθιάδ' ἀντὶ Δωρικῆς
οἴσει τις ἡμῖν κοπίδ', ἀπορρήξω χέλυν;
λαβὼν δὲ κόπτει. σπλάγχνα δ' Αἴγισθος λαβὼν
ἤθρει διαιρῶν. τοῦ δὲ νεύοντος κάτω
ὄνυχας ἐπ' ἄκρους στὰς κασίγνητος σέθεν   840

76

do badly"—he meant you and Orestes.
My master prayed for quite the opposite,
not saying the words aloud, so he might win
his ancestral home. Then from a basket   [810]
Aegisthus took a sacrificial knife,
sliced off some of the calf's hair, and set it
with his right hand on the sacred fire.
His servants raised the calf onto their shoulders,
he cut its throat and spoke out to your brother,
"People claim this about men from Thessaly—
they're exceptional at butchering bulls
as well as taming horses. So, stranger,
take this knife and demonstrate to us
if that report about Thessalians is true."
Orestes gripped the well-made Dorian knife,
tossed from his shoulders his fine-looking cloak,   [820]
and chose Pylades to help him in the work.
Pushing slaves aside, he took the calf's hoof,
and, stretching out his arms, cut open
the beast's white flesh and then stripped off the hide
faster than any runner could complete
two circuits on a track for racing horses.
He opened up the flanks, and Aegisthus
picked up the sacred entrails in his hands
to have a look at them. But on the liver
the lobe was missing. There were signs of damage
which the man inspecting them could see
close to the gall bladder and the portal vein.
Aegisthus was upset. My master asked,   [830]
"Why are you upset?" "Stranger," he replied,
"what I'm afraid of is foreign treachery.
Most of all I hate Agamemnon's son,
an enemy of my house." My master said,
"Do you really fear an exile's trickery,
you, lord of the city? Let someone bring me,
a Phthian axe to replace this Doric knife
and let me split apart the breast bone,
so we can feast upon the inner organs."
He took the axe and struck. Then Aegisthus
picked up and separated out the innards
and peered at them. As he was bending down,
your brother, standing on tip toe, hit him   [840]

Euripides

ἐς σφονδύλους ἔπαισε, νωτιαῖα δὲ
ἔρρηξεν ἄρθρα· πᾶν δὲ σῶμ' ἄνω κάτω
ἤσπαιρεν ἠλάλαζε δυσθνῄσκων φόνῳ.
δμῶες δ' ἰδόντες εὐθὺς ᾖξαν ἐς δόρυ,
πολλοὶ μάχεσθαι πρὸς δύ'· ἀνδρείας δ' ὕπο   845
ἔστησαν ἀντίπρῳρα σείοντες βέλη
Πυλάδης Ὀρέστης τ'. εἶπε δ'· Οὐχὶ δυσμενὴς
ἥκω πόλει τῇδ' οὐδ' ἐμοῖς ὁπάοσιν,
φονέα δὲ πατρὸς ἀντετιμωρησάμην
τλήμων Ὀρέστης· ἀλλὰ μή με καίνετε,   850
πατρὸς παλαιοὶ δμῶες. οἳ δ', ἐπεὶ λόγων
ἤκουσαν, ἔσχον κάμακας· ἐγνώσθη δ' ὑπὸ
γέροντος ἐν δόμοισιν ἀρχαίου τινός.
στέφουσι δ' εὐθὺς σοῦ κασιγνήτου κάρα
χαίροντες ἀλαλάζοντες. ἔρχεται δὲ σοὶ   855
κάρα 'πιδείξων οὐχὶ Γοργόνος φέρων,
ἀλλ' ὃν στυγεῖς Αἴγισθον· αἷμα δ' αἵματος
πικρὸς δανεισμὸς ἦλθε τῷ θανόντι νῦν.

ΧΟΡΟΣ

θὲς ἐς χορόν, ὦ φίλα, ἴχνος,   860
ὡς νεβρὸς οὐράνιον
πήδημα κουφίζουσα σὺν ἀγλαΐᾳ.
νικᾷ στεφαναφορίαν
† κρείσσω τοῖς † παρ' Ἀλφειοῦ ῥεέθροισι τελέσσας
κασίγνητος σέθεν· ἀλλ' ἐπάειδε
καλλίνικον ᾠδὰν ἐμῷ χορῷ.   865

ΗΛΕΚΤΡΑ

ὦ φέγγος, ὦ τέθριππον ἡλίου σέλας,
ὦ γαῖα καὶ νὺξ ἣν ἐδερκόμην πάρος,
νῦν ὄμμα τοὐμὸν ἀμπτυχαί τ' ἐλεύθεροι,
ἐπεὶ πατρὸς πέπτωκεν Αἴγισθος φονεύς.

78

on the spine and cut through his vertebrae.
His whole body went into convulsions,
shaking up and down, and he kept screaming,
he was dying in his own blood, a brutal death.
The servants saw and rushed to get their spears
for a fight of many men against just two.
But Pylades and Orestes stood there,
brandishing their weapons with great courage.
Then my master said, "I have not come here
as an enemy, not to the city
or my servants, but to avenge myself
on the man who murdered my own father.
I am unfortunate Orestes. You men,   [850]
old servants of my father, don't kill me."
After the servants heard Orestes' words,
they pulled back their spears. Then an old man
who'd been a long time in the household
recognized him. At once they placed a wreath
on your brother's head, shouting and rejoicing,
and he's coming here carrying a head
to show it to you—not the Gorgon's head,
but from the person you so hate, Aegisthus.
So the bitter debt of murderous bloodshed
is paid by the man who's just been slaughtered.

[The Messenger leaves]

CHORUS
O my friend, set your feet to dancing,
leaping nimbly up to heaven with joy.   [860]
Your brother has emerged victorious
and now he's won himself a crown,
in a competition surpassing those
which happen by Alpheus' streams.[23]
Come, as I perform my dance
sing out a song of glorious victory.

ELECTRA
O light! O blazing chariot of the sun!
O earth and night whom I gazed at before!
I've freedom now to open up my eyes—
Aegisthus, the man who killed my father,

φέρ᾽, οἷα δὴ ἔχω καὶ δόμοι κεύθουσί μου 870
κόμης ἀγάλματ᾽ ἐξενέγκωμαι, φίλαι,
στέψω τ᾽ ἀδελφοῦ κρᾶτα τοῦ νικηφόρου.

ΧΟΡΟΣ

σὺ μέν νυν ἀγάλματ᾽ ἄειρε
κρατί· τὸ δ᾽ ἀμέτερον
χωρήσεται Μούσαισι χόρευμα φίλον. 875
νῦν οἱ πάρος ἀμέτεροι
γαίας τυραννεύσουσι φίλοι βασιλῆες,
δικαίως ... τοὺς δ᾽ ἀδίκως καθελόντες.
ἀλλ᾽ ἴτω ξύναυλος βυὰ χαρᾷ.

ΗΛΕΚΤΡΑ

ὦ καλλίνικε, πατρὸς ἐκ νικηφόρου 880
γεγώς, Ὀρέστα, τῆς ὑπ᾽ Ἰλίῳ μάχης,
δέξαι κόμης σῆς βοστρύχων ἀνδήματα.
ἥκεις γὰρ οὐκ ἀχρεῖον ἔκπλεθρον δραμὼν
ἀγῶν᾽ ἐς οἴκους, ἀλλὰ πολέμιον κτανὼν
Αἴγισθον, ὃς σὸν πατέρα κἀμὸν ὤλεσε. 885
σύ τ᾽, ὦ παρασπίστ᾽, ἀνδρὸς εὐσεβεστάτου
παίδευμα Πυλάδη, στέφανον ἐξ ἐμῆς χερὸς
δέχου· φέρῃ γὰρ καὶ σὺ τῷδ᾽ ἴσον μέρος
ἀγῶνος· αἰεὶ δ᾽ εὐτυχεῖς φαίνοισθέ μοι.

ΟΡΕΣΤΗΣ

θεοὺς μὲν ἡγοῦ πρῶτον, Ἠλέκτρα, τύχης 890
ἀρχηγέτας τῆσδ᾽, εἶτα κἄμ᾽ ἐπαίνεσον
τὸν τῶν θεῶν τε τῆς τύχης θ᾽ ὑπηρέτην.
ἥκω γὰρ οὐ λόγοισιν ἀλλ᾽ ἔργοις κτανὼν
Αἴγισθον· ὡς δὲ τῷ σάφ᾽ εἰδέναι τάδε
προσθῶμεν, αὐτὸν τὸν θανόντα σοι φέρω, 895
ὃν εἴτε χρῄζεις θηρσὶν ἁρπαγὴν πρόθες,
ἢ σκῦλον οἰωνοῖσιν, αἰθέρος τέκνοις,
πήξασ᾽ ἔρεισον σκόλοπι· σὸς γάρ ἐστι νῦν
[δοῦλος, πάροιθε δεσπότης κεκλημένος.]

is fallen. Come, my friends, let's bring out [870]
whatever I keep stored up in the house
as decorations for my brother's hair.
I'll make a crown for his triumphant head.

CHORUS

Bring on your decorations for his head.
and we'll keep up the dance the Muses love.
Now those dear kings we had before
will rule this land of ours with justice.
They've cast down those who broke our laws.
So let's sing out in joyful harmony.

[Orestes and Pylades enter with their attendants, who are carrying the body of Aegisthus]

ELECTRA

O Orestes, you glorious conqueror, [880]
born from a father who was victorious
in the war at Troy. Take these ribbons
for your locks of hair. You've come back home,
and your run around the stadium racetrack
has not been in vain. You've killed Aegisthus,
the man who killed our father, yours and mine,
our enemy. And you, who stood by him,
Pylades, reared by a pious father,
receive from my own hand this wreath. Your share
in this competition matched Orestes.
I hope I see you always prospering.

ORESTES

First of all, Electra, you must believe [890]
the gods were leaders in what's happened here.
Then praise me as a servant of the gods
and circumstance. I have returned back home
and killed Aegisthus, not in word but deed.
To underscore the truth of what I've said,
I've carried out the dead man's corpse for you.
If it's what you want, lay him out as prey
for wild beasts or impale him on a stake,
a prize for birds, those children of the sky.
In earlier days he was called your master,
and now he is your slave.

ΗΛΕΚΤΡΑ

αἰσχύνομαι μέν, βούλομαι δ' εἰπεῖν ὅμως.　　　900

ΟΡΕΣΤΗΣ

τί χρῆμα; λέξον· ὡς φόβου γ' ἔξωθεν εἶ.

ΗΛΕΚΤΡΑ

νεκροὺς ὑβρίζειν, μή μέ τις φθόνῳ βάλῃ.

ΟΡΕΣΤΗΣ

οὐκ ἔστιν οὐδεὶς ὅστις ἂν μέμψαιτό σε.

ΗΛΕΚΤΡΑ

δυσάρεστος ἡμῶν καὶ φιλόψογος πόλις.

ΟΡΕΣΤΗΣ

λέγ', εἴ τι χρῄζεις, σύγγον'· ἀσπόνδοισι γὰρ　　　905
νόμοισιν ἔχθραν τῷδε συμβεβλήκαμεν.

ΗΛΕΚΤΡΑ

εἶέν· τίν' ἀρχὴν πρῶτά σ' ἐξείπω κακῶν,
ποίας τελευτάς; τίνα μέσον τάξω λόγον;
καὶ μὴν δι' ὄρθρων γ' οὔποτ' ἐξελίμπανον
θρυλοῦσ' ἅ γ' εἰπεῖν ἤθελον κατ' ὄμμα σόν,　　　910
εἰ δὴ γενοίμην δειμάτων ἐλευθέρα
τῶν πρόσθε. νῦν οὖν ἐσμεν· ἀποδώσω δέ σοι
ἐκεῖν' ἅ σε ζῶντ' ἤθελον λέξαι κακά.
ἀπώλεσάς με κὠρφανὴν φίλου πατρὸς
καὶ τόνδ' ἔθηκας, οὐδὲν ἠδικημένος,　　　915
κἄγημας αἰσχρῶς μητέρ' ἄνδρα τ' ἔκτανες
στρατηλατοῦνθ' Ἕλλησιν, οὐκ ἐλθὼν Φρύγας.
ἐς τοῦτο δ' ἦλθες ἀμαθίας ὥστ' ἤλπισας
ὡς ἐς σὲ ἐμὴν δὴ μητέρ' οὐχ ἕξοις κακὴν

ELECTRA

                        I feel ashamed,   [900]
but nonetheless I wish to speak.

ORESTES

                              What is it?
Speak up. There's nothing you need to fear.

ELECTRA

    To insult the dead — in case someone
might heap reproaches on me.

ORESTES

                      But no one
would blame you in the slightest.

ELECTRA

                          But the city
is hard to please and loves to criticize.

ORESTES

    Speak, sister, if you want to say something.
We are his enemies — there are no rules
in our relationship with him.

ELECTRA *[to the corpse of Aegisthus]*

                        Well, then,
how shall I first begin to speak about
the evil you have done? Where do I end?
What words shall I use for the central part?
It's true that in the dawn I never stopped
rehearsing what I wished to say to you,
right to your face, if I were ever free
from my old fears. Well, now I am free.   [910]
So I will pay you back, abusing you
the way I wanted to when you were living.
You ruined me, taking away from me
and from this man here our dear father,
although we hadn't done you any wrong.
You made a shameful marriage with my mother,
then killed her husband, who was the general
who led the Greeks. You never went to Troy.
And you were so idiotic you believed
that with my mother you would get a wife

83

γήμας, ἐμοῦ δὲ πατρὸς ἠδίκεις λέχη.   920
ἴστω δ᾽, ὅταν τις διολέσας δάμαρτά του
κρυπταῖσιν εὐναῖς εἶτ᾽ ἀναγκασθῇ λαβεῖν,
δύστηνός ἐστιν, εἰ δοκεῖ τὸ σωφρονεῖν
ἐκεῖ μὲν αὐτὴν οὐκ ἔχειν, παρ᾽ οἷ δ᾽ ἔχειν.
ἄλγιστα δ᾽ ᾤκεις, οὐ δοκῶν οἰκεῖν κακῶς·   925
ᾔδησθα γὰρ δῆτ᾽ ἀνόσιον γήμας γάμον,
μήτηρ δὲ σ᾽ ἄνδρα δυσσεβῆ κεκτημένη.
ἄμφω πονηρὼ δ᾽ ὄντ᾽ ἀφαιρεῖσθον τύχην
† κείνη τε τὴν σὴν καὶ σὺ τοὐκείνης κακόν. †
πᾶσιν δ᾽ ἐν Ἀργείοισιν ἤκουες τάδε·   930
Ὁ τῆς γυναικός—οὐχὶ τἀνδρὸς ἡ γυνή.
καίτοι τόδ᾽ αἰσχρόν, προστατεῖν γε δωμάτων
γυναῖκα, μὴ τὸν ἄνδρα· κἀκείνους στυγῶ
τοὺς παῖδας, ὅστις τοῦ μὲν ἄρσενος πατρὸς
οὐκ ὠνόμασται, τῆς δὲ μητρὸς ἐν πόλει.   935
ἐπίσημα γὰρ γήμαντι καὶ μείζω λέχη
τἀνδρὸς μὲν οὐδείς, τῶν δὲ θηλειῶν λόγος.
ὃ δ᾽ ἠπάτα σε πλεῖστον οὐκ ἐγνωκότα,
ηὔχεις τις εἶναι τοῖσι χρήμασι σθένων·
τὰ δ᾽ οὐδὲν εἰ μὴ βραχὺν ὁμιλῆσαι χρόνον.   940
ἡ γὰρ φύσις βέβαιος, οὐ τὰ χρήματα.
ἣ μὲν γὰρ αἰεὶ παραμένουσ᾽ αἴρει κακά·
ὁ δ᾽ ὄλβος ἀδίκως καὶ μετὰ σκαιῶν ξυνὼν
ἐξέπτατ᾽ οἴκων, σμικρὸν ἀνθήσας χρόνον.
ἃ δ᾽ ἐς γυναῖκας—παρθένῳ γὰρ οὐ καλὸν   945
λέγειν—σιωπῶ, γνωρίμως δ᾽ αἰνίξομαι.
ὕβριζες, ὡς δὴ βασιλικοὺς ἔχων δόμους
κάλλει τ᾽ ἀραρώς. ἀλλ᾽ ἔμοιγ᾽ εἴη πόσις
μὴ παρθενωπός, ἀλλὰ τἀνδρείου τρόπου.
τὰ γὰρ τέκν᾽ αὐτῶν Ἄρεος ἐκκρεμάννυται,   950

who was not evil, though she was betraying   [920]
my father's bed. But you must know this—
when any man corrupts another's wife,
having sex with her in secret, and then
is compelled to take her as his wife,
such a man is foolish if he believes
that, though she was not virtuous before,
she will be now with him. You were living
an agonizing life, although it seemed
as if the way you lived was not so bad.
You knew well you'd made a profane marriage.
My mother realized she had in you
a sacrilegious man. You are both evil,
and so you both acquired each other's traits.
She shares your wickedness, and you share hers.
You heard these words from all the Argives—   [930]
"That woman's husband," not "that man's wife."
And this is truly shameful—when the wife
controls the home rather than the husband.
I hate those offspring whom the city calls
children of their mother instead of saying
sons of their father. Still, when any man
makes a distinguished marriage well above
his station, no one talks of him,
but only of his wife. But most of all,
you were so ignorant you were deceived
in claiming to be someone because your strength
was in your wealth. But that's not worth a thing—   [940]
its presence is short lived. What stays secure
is nature, not possessions. It stands there,
beside you, and takes away your troubles.
But when riches live with fools unjustly,
they bloom a little while, then flee the house.
As for your women, I will say nothing—
it's not good a virgin speak about such things.
But I'll provide a hint, a simple riddle.
You were abusive, with your royal home,
your seductive looks. May I never have
a husband with the face of a young girl,
but one who has the look of a real man.
His children hold onto a life of war.   [950]

τὰ δ' εὐπρεπῆ δὴ κόσμος ἐν χοροῖς μόνον.
ἔρρ', οὐδὲν εἰδὼς ὧν ἐφευρεθεὶς χρόνῳ
δίκην δέδωκας. —ὧδέ τις κακοῦργος ὢν
μή μοι τὸ πρῶτον βῆμ' ἐὰν δράμῃ καλῶς,
νικᾶν δοκείτω τὴν Δίκην, πρὶν ἂν πέλας   955
γραμμῆς ἵκηται καὶ τέλος κάμψῃ βίου.

ΧΟΡΟΣ
ἔπραξε δεινά, δεινὰ δ' ἀντέδωκε σοὶ
καὶ τῷδ'· ἔχει γὰρ ἡ Δίκη μέγα σθένος.

ΗΛΕΚΤΡΑ
εἶέν· κομίζειν τοῦδε σῶμ' ἔσω χρεὼν
σκότῳ τε δοῦναι, δμῶες, ὡς, ὅταν μόλῃ   960
μήτηρ, σφαγῆς πάροιθε μὴ εἰσίδῃ νεκρόν.

ΟΡΕΣΤΗΣ
ἐπίσχες· ἐμβάλωμεν εἰς ἄλλον λόγον.

ΗΛΕΚΤΡΑ
τί δ'; ἐκ Μυκηνῶν μῶν βοηδρόμους ὁρῶ;

ΟΡΕΣΤΗΣ
οὔκ, ἀλλὰ τὴν τεκοῦσαν ἥ μ' ἐγείνατο.

ΗΛΕΚΤΡΑ
καλῶς ἄρ' ἄρκυν ἐς μέσην πορεύεται . . .   965
καὶ μὴν ὄχοις γε καὶ στολῇ λαμπρύνεται.

ΟΡΕΣΤΗΣ
τί δῆτα δρῶμεν μητέρ'; ἦ φονεύσομεν;

ΗΛΕΚΤΡΑ
μῶν σ' οἶκτος εἷλε, μητρὸς ὡς εἶδες δέμας;

The pretty ones are only ornaments
to decorate the dancing choruses.
So get out of here, and stay ignorant
how you were found in time and punished.
And let no man committing wicked acts
believe that, if he runs the first lap well,
he is defeating justice, not before
he get to the finish, when he completes
the last turn in his life.

CHORUS LEADER

      What this man's done
is dreadful, and he's paid a dreadful price
to you and to Orestes. For Justice
has a power that's enormous.

ELECTRA

 Well, you servants must take up the body
and hide it inside, somewhere in the dark,   [960]
so when my mother comes over here
she won't see his corpse before she's killed.

[Pylades and the attendants take Aegisthus' body into the house]

ORESTES *[looking off stage]*
 Wait a moment. Here's another thing
we need to deal with.

ELECTRA

      What? Are those men I see
reinforcements coming from Mycenae?

ORESTES
 No. That's the mother who gave birth to me.

ELECTRA
 She's moving neatly right into our net.
How splendid she looks in that carriage,
such fine clothes.

ORESTES

      What are we going to do?
Kill our mother?

ELECTRA

     You're not overcome with pity
now you've seen our mother in the flesh?

ΟΡΕΣΤΗΣ

φεῦ·

πῶς γὰρ κτάνω νιν, ἥ μ' ἔθρεψε κἄτεκεν;

ΗΛΕΚΤΡΑ

ὥσπερ πατέρα σὸν ἥδε κἀμὸν ὤλεσεν.   970

ΟΡΕΣΤΗΣ

ὦ Φοῖβε, πολλήν γ' ἀμαθίαν ἐθέσπισας . . .

ΗΛΕΚΤΡΑ

ὅπου δ' Ἀπόλλων σκαιὸς ᾖ, τίνες σοφοί;

ΟΡΕΣΤΗΣ

ὅστις μ' ἔχρησας μητέρ', ἣν οὐ χρῆν, κτανεῖν.

ΗΛΕΚΤΡΑ

βλάπτῃ δὲ δὴ τί πατρὶ τιμωρῶν σέθεν;

ΟΡΕΣΤΗΣ

μητροκτόνος νῦν φεύξομαι, τόθ' ἁγνὸς ὤν.   975

ΗΛΕΚΤΡΑ

καὶ μή γ' ἀμύνων πατρὶ δυσσεβὴς ἔσῃ.

ΟΡΕΣΤΗΣ

ἐγὼ δὲ μητρὸς —; τῷ φόνου δώσω δίκας;

ΗΛΕΚΤΡΑ

τῷ δ' ἢν πατρῴαν διαμεθῇς τιμωρίαν;

ΟΡΕΣΤΗΣ

ἆρ' αὖτ' ἀλάστωρ εἶπ' ἀπεικασθεὶς θεῷ;

ΗΛΕΚΤΡΑ

ἱερὸν καθίζων τρίποδ'; ἐγὼ μὲν οὐ δοκῶ.   980

ORESTES
Ah, how can I kill her? She gave birth to me.
She raised me.

ELECTRA
                    Just as she killed our father,   [970]
yours and mine.

ORESTES
                              O Phoebus Apollo,
that prophecy of yours was so foolish.[24]

ELECTRA
Where Apollo is a fool, what men are wise?

ORESTES
You instructed me to kill my mother,
but killing her is wrong.

ELECTRA
                    On the other hand,
if you're avenging your own father
how can you be harmed?

ORESTES
                              I'll be prosecuted
for slaughtering my mother. Before now
I've been free of all impiety.

ELECTRA
But if you don't defend your father,
you're a guilty man.

ORESTES
                    But my mother?
If I kill her, how will I be punished?

ELECTRA
What will happen to you if you give up
avenging your own father?

ORESTES
                    Could it have been
a demon in the likeness of a god
who spoke?

ELECTRA
                    Sitting on the sacred tripod?   [980]
I don't think so.

ΟΡΕΣΤΗΣ

οὐδ' ἂν πιθοίμην εὖ μεμαντεῦσθαι τάδε.

ΗΛΕΚΤΡΑ

οὐ μὴ κακισθεὶς εἰς ἀνανδρίαν πεσῇ.

ΟΡΕΣΤΗΣ

ἀλλ' ἦ τὸν αὐτὸν τῇδ' ὑποστήσω δόλον;

ΗΛΕΚΤΡΑ

ᾧ καὶ πόσιν καθεῖλες, Αἴγισθον κτανών.

ΟΡΕΣΤΗΣ

ἔσειμι· δεινοῦ δ' ἄρχομαι προβλήματος   985
καὶ δεινὰ δράσω γε—εἰ θεοῖς δοκεῖ τάδε,
ἔστω· πικρὸν δὲ χἠδὺ τἀγώνισμά μοι.

ΧΟΡΟΣ

[ἰώ,]
βασίλεια γύναι χθονὸς Ἀργείας,
παῖ Τυνδάρεω,
καὶ τοῖν ἀγαθοῖν ξύγγονε κούροιν   990
Διός, οἳ φλογερὰν αἰθέρ' ἐν ἄστροις
ναίουσι, βροτῶν ἐν ἁλὸς ῥοθίοις
    τιμὰς σωτῆρας ἔχοντες·
χαῖρε, σεβίζω σ' ἴσα καὶ μάκαρας
πλούτου μεγάλης τ' εὐδαιμονίας.   995
τὰς σὰς δὲ τύχας θεραπεύεσθαι
    καιρός. ⟨χαῖρ',⟩ ὦ βασίλεια.

ΚΛΥΤΑΙΜΗΣΤΡΑ

ἔκβητ' ἀπήνης, Τρῳάδες, χειρὸς δ' ἐμῆς
λάβεσθ', ἵν' ἔξω τοῦδ' ὄχου στήσω πόδα.
σκύλοισι μὲν γὰρ θεῶν κεκόσμηνται δόμοι   1000
Φρυγίοις, ἐγὼ δὲ τάσδε, Τρῳάδος χθονὸς
ἐξαίρετ', ἀντὶ παιδὸς ἣν ἀπώλεσα
σμικρὸν γέρας, καλὸν δὲ κέκτημαι δόμοις.

ORESTES

                     I cannot believe
this prophecy was good.

ELECTRA

                     You must be a man.
Don't give way to cowardice. Set for her
the same trap you used to kill her husband,
when you destroyed Aegisthus.

ORESTES

                     I'll go in.
I'm about to launch a terrible act
and do dreadful things. Well, so be it,
if the gods approve of this. But to me
this contest is a bitter one, not sweet.

[Orestes goes into the house. Clytaemnestra arrives in a chariot with attendants]

CHORUS

Greetings lady, child of Tyndareus,
queen of this country of the Argives,
sister of those noble twins,   [990]
Zeus' sons, who live in heaven
among the fiery constellations
and have the honourable task
of saving mortals in the roaring waves.[25]
Welcome! I worship you
no less than I revere the gods
for your great wealth and happiness.
My queen, it's now appropriate
that we attend to your good fortunes.

CLYTAEMNESTRA

Get down from the carriage, women of Troy,
and take my hand, so I, too, may step down
out of this wagon. The houses of the gods   [1000]
may be adorned with Phrygian trophies,
but I obtained these female slaves from Troy,
the finest in the land, as ornaments
within my household, small compensation
for the child I lost.[26]

ΗΛΕΚΤΡΑ

οὔκουν ἐγώ—δούλη γὰρ ἐκβεβλημένη
δόμων πατρῴων δυστυχεῖς οἰκῶ δόμους—   1005
μῆτερ, λάβωμαι μακαρίας τῆς σῆς χερός;

ΚΛΥΤΑΙΜΗΣΤΡΑ

δοῦλαι πάρεισιν αἵδε, μὴ σύ μοι πόνει.

ΗΛΕΚΤΡΑ

τί δ'; αἰχμάλωτόν τοί μ' ἀπῴκισας δόμων,
ἠρημένων δὲ δωμάτων ἠρήμεθα,
ὡς αἵδε, πατρὸς ὀρφαναὶ λελειμμέναι.   1010

ΚΛΥΤΑΙΜΗΣΤΡΑ

τοιαῦτα μέντοι σὸς πατὴρ βουλεύματα
ἐς οὓς ἐχρῆν ἥκιστ' ἐβούλευσεν φίλων.
λέξω δὲ ... καίτοι δόξ' ὅταν λάβῃ κακὴ
γυναῖκα, γλώσσῃ πικρότης ἔνεστί τις.
ὡς μὲν παρ' ἡμῖν, οὐ καλῶς· τὸ πρᾶγμα δὲ   1015
μαθόντας, ἢν μὲν ἀξίως μισεῖν ἔχῃς,
στυγεῖν δίκαιον· εἰ δὲ μή, τί δεῖ στυγεῖν;
ἡμᾶς ἔδωκε Τυνδάρεως τῷ σῷ πατρί,
οὐχ ὥστε θνῄσκειν, οὐδ' ἃ γειναίμην ἐγώ.
κεῖνος δὲ παῖδα τὴν ἐμὴν Ἀχιλλέως   1020
λέκτροισι πείσας ᾤχετ' ἐκ δόμων ἄγων
πρυμνοῦχον Αὖλιν, ἔνθ' ὑπερτείνας πυρᾶς
λευκὴν διήμησ' Ἰφιγόνης παρηΐδα.
κεἰ μὲν πόλεως ἅλωσιν ἐξιώμενος,
ἢ δῶμ' ὀνήσων τἄλλα τ' ἐκσῴζων τέκνα,   1025
ἔκτεινε πολλῶν μίαν ὕπερ, συγγνώστ' ἂν ἦν·
νῦν δ' οὕνεχ' Ἑλένη μάργος ἦν ὅ τ' αὖ λαβὼν
ἄλοχον κολάζειν προδότιν οὐκ ἠπίστατο,
τούτων ἕκατι παῖδ' ἐμὴν διώλεσεν.

92

ELECTRA

                    Mother, is it all right
for me to take that blessed hand of yours,
given I live in this decrepit house,
just like a slave, now I've been cast out
of my ancestral home?

CLYTAEMNESTRA

                  The slaves are here.
Don't exert yourself on my behalf.

ELECTRA

Why not? After all, I'm a captive, too,
you sent away from home. Like these women,
I was taken when my house was seized   [1010]
and left without a father.

CLYTAEMNESTRA

               Well, your father
brought that about with plots against the ones
he should have loved the most, his own family.
I'll describe it to you, though when a woman
gets an evil name, her tongue grows bitter,
and that, it seems to me, is no bad thing.
But you should learn the facts of what's gone on
and then despise it, if it's worth your hate.
If not, why hate at all? Tyndareus
gave me to your father, not intending
that I or any children I might bear
should die. But that man, when he left his home,   [1020]
convinced my daughter to accompany him,
by promising a marriage with Achilles,
and took her to the anchored fleet at Aulis.[27]
There he had Iphigeneia stretched out
and slit her pale white throat above the fire.
If he'd killed one girl for the sake of many,
to protect the city from being taken,
or to help his house or save his family,
I'd have pardoned him. But he killed my child
because of Helen's lust, because the man
who'd taken her as wife had no idea
how to keep his treacherous mate controlled.

Euripides

ἐπὶ τοῖσδε τοίνυν καίπερ ἠδικημένη   1030
οὐκ ἠγριώμην οὐδ' ἂν ἔκτανον πόσιν·
ἀλλ' ἦλθ' ἔχων μοι μαινάδ' ἔνθεον κόρην
λέκτροις τ' ἐπεισέφρηκε, καὶ νύμφα δύο
ἐν τοῖσιν αὐτοῖς δώμασιν κατείχομεν.
μῶρον μὲν οὖν γυναῖκες, οὐκ ἄλλως λέγω·   1035
ὅταν δ', ὑπόντος τοῦδ', ἁμαρτάνῃ πόσις
τἄνδον παρώσας λέκτρα, μιμεῖσθαι θέλει
γυνὴ τὸν ἄνδρα χἄτερον κτᾶσθαι φίλον.
κἄπειτ' ἐν ἡμῖν ὁ ψόγος λαμπρύνεται,
οἱ δ' αἴτιοι τῶνδ' οὐ κλύουσ' ἄνδρες κακῶς.   1040
εἰ δ' ἐκ δόμων ἥρπαστο Μενέλεως λάθρᾳ,
κτανεῖν μ' Ὀρέστην χρῆν, κασιγνήτης πόσιν
Μενέλαον ὡς σώσαιμι; σὸς δὲ πῶς πατὴρ
ἠνέσχετ' ἂν ταῦτ'; εἶτα τὸν μὲν οὐ θανεῖν
κτείνοντα χρῆν τἄμ', ἐμὲ δὲ πρὸς κείνου παθεῖν;   1045
ἔκτειν', ἐτρέφθην ἥνπερ ἦν πορεύσιμον
πρὸς τοὺς ἐκείνῳ πολεμίους. φίλων γὰρ ἂν
τίς ἂν πατρὸς σοῦ φόνον ἐκοινώνησέ μοι;
λέγ', εἴ τι χρῄζεις, κἀντίθες παρρησίᾳ,
ὅπως τέθνηκε σὸς πατὴρ οὐκ ἐνδίκως.   1050

ΧΟΡΟΣ
δίκαι' ἔλεξας· ἡ δίκη δ' αἰσχρῶς ἔχει.
γυναῖκα γὰρ χρὴ πάντα συγχωρεῖν πόσει,
ἥτις φρενήρης· ᾗ δὲ μὴ δοκεῖ τάδε,
οὐδ' εἰς ἀριθμὸν τῶν ἐμῶν ἥκει λόγων.

ΗΛΕΚΤΡΑ
μέμνησο, μῆτερ, οὓς ἔλεξας ὑστάτους   1055
λόγους, διδοῦσα πρός σέ μοι παρρησίαν.

ΚΛΥΤΑΙΜΗΣΤΡΑ
καὶ νῦν γέ φημι κοὐκ ἀπαρνοῦμαι, τέκνον.

ΗΛΕΚΤΡΑ
† ἆρα † κλύουσα, μῆτερ, εἶτ' ἔρξεις κακῶς;

94

For all of that, although I had been wronged,   [1030]
I'd not have grown enraged or killed my husband.
But he came back to me with some mad girl—
possessed by gods—and put her in his bed,
so he could have two brides in the same house.²⁸
Women are foolish. I'll concede the point.
But given that, when a husband goes astray,
rejecting his domestic bed, his wife
may well wish to follow his example
and find another man to love. And then
the blame makes us notorious—the men
who caused it all are never criticized.   [1040]
If someone had carried Menelaus
away from home in secret, should I then
have killed Orestes to save Menelaus,
my sister's husband? How would your father
have put up with that? So is it not right
for him to die? He slaughtered my own child.
I would've kept on suffering at his hands.
I killed him. The road lay open to me,
and so I turned towards his enemies.
After all, which one of your father's friends
would have joined me to commit the murder?
Speak up, if you wish, and answer frankly.
In what way was your father's death unjust?   [1050]

CHORUS LEADER
There's justice in your words, but that justice
is disgraceful. If she has any sense,
a woman should give way in everything
to her own husband. Those who disagree
I don't take into account in things I say.

ELECTRA
Bear in mind, mother, the last thing you said,
offering me a chance to be frank with you.

CLYTAEMNESTRA
Yes, my child. And I won't take that back.
I'll repeat it now.

ELECTRA
                    You'll hear me out, mother,
and won't punish me?

ΚΛΥΤΑΙΜΗΣΤΡΑ
οὐκ ἔστι, τῇ σῇ δ' ἡδὺ προσθήσω φρενί.

ΗΛΕΚΤΡΑ
λέγοιμ' ἄν· ἀρχὴ δ' ἥδε μοι προοιμίου·   1060
εἴθ' εἶχες, ὦ τεκοῦσα, βελτίους φρένας.
τὸ μὲν γὰρ εἶδος αἶνον ἄξιον φέρειν
Ἑλένης τε καὶ σοῦ, δύο δ' ἔφυτε συγγόνω,
ἄμφω ματαίω Κάστορός τ' οὐκ ἀξίω.
ἡ μὲν γὰρ ἁρπασθεῖσ' ἑκοῦσ' ἀπώλετο,   1065
σὺ δ' ἄνδρ' ἄριστον Ἑλλάδος διώλεσας,
σκῆψιν προτείνουσ', ὡς ὑπὲρ τέκνου πόσιν
ἔκτεινας· οὐ γάρ σ' ὡς ἔγωγ' ἴσασιν εὖ.
ἥτις, θυγατρὸς πρὶν κεκυρῶσθαι σφαγάς,
νέον τ' ἀπ' οἴκων ἀνδρὸς ἐξωρμημένου,   1070
ξανθὸν κατόπτρῳ πλόκαμον ἐξήσκεις κόμης.
γυνὴ δ', ἀπόντος ἀνδρός, ἥτις ἐκ δόμων
ἐς κάλλος ἀσκεῖ, διάγραφ' ὡς οὖσαν κακήν.
οὐδὲν γὰρ αὐτὴν δεῖ θύρασιν εὐπρεπὲς
φαίνειν πρόσωπον, ἤν τι μὴ ζητῇ κακόν.   1075
μόνη δὲ πασῶν οἶδ' ἐγὼ σ' Ἑλληνίδων,
εἰ μὲν τὰ Τρώων εὐτυχοῖ, κεχαρμένην,
εἰ δ' ἧσσον' εἴη, συννεφοῦσαν ὄμματα,
Ἀγαμέμνον' οὐ χρῄζουσαν ἐκ Τροίας μολεῖν.
καίτοι καλῶς γε σωφρονεῖν παρεῖχέ σοι·   1080
ἄνδρ' εἶχες οὐ κακίον' Αἰγίσθου πόσιν,
ὃν Ἑλλὰς αὑτῆς εἵλετο στρατηλάτην·
Ἑλένης δ' ἀδελφῆς τοιάδ' ἐξειργασμένης
ἐξῆν κλέος σοι μέγα λαβεῖν· τὰ γὰρ κακὰ
παράδειγμα τοῖς ἐσθλοῖσιν εἴσοψίν τ' ἔχει.   1085
εἰ δ', ὡς λέγεις, σὴν θυγατέρ' ἔκτεινεν πατήρ,
ἐγὼ τί σ' ἠδίκησ' ἐμός τε σύγγονος;

CLYTAEMNESTRA

                    No, I won't,
not if I'm giving pleasure to your heart.

ELECTRA

Then I'll speak, starting with an opening comment.   [1060]
O mother, I do wish you had more sense.
Your beauty brings you praise that's well deserved—
the same is true for Helen—but you two
were born twin sisters, both very silly,
quite unworthy of your brother Castor.
She was willing to be carried off and ruined,
and you destroyed the finest man in Greece,
using the excuse you killed your husband
for your child, since people do not know you
the way I do. But before it was decided
that your daughter would be sacrificed,   [1070]
no sooner had your husband left his home,
than you were fixing your fine locks of hair
seated at your mirror, and any wife
who primps her beauty when her husband's gone,
you can scratch her off the list as worthless.
There's no call for her to show her pretty face
outside the home, unless she's seeking mischief.
Of all the women in Greece, I believe
you were the only one who was happy
whenever Trojan fortunes were successful
and whose eyes would frown when they got worse,
because it was your hope that Agamemnon
would not get back from Troy. But nonetheless,
you could have stayed a truly virtuous woman.   [1080]
The husband you had was in no way worse
than that Aegisthus, and he'd been chosen
by the Greeks themselves to lead the army.
When your sister Helen did what she did,
you had an opportunity to gain
great glory for yourself, since bad conduct
sets a standard for our noble actions
and makes them something everyone can see.
But if, as you are claiming, our father
killed your daughter, how have you been wronged
by me and by my brother? Why is it,

πῶς οὐ πόσιν κτείνασα πατρῴους δόμους
ἡμῖν προσῆψας, ἀλλ᾽ ἐπηνέγκω λέχει
τἀλλότρια, μισθοῦ τοὺς γάμους ὠνουμένη;   1090
κοὔτ᾽ ἀντιφεύγει παιδὸς ἀντὶ σοῦ πόσις,
οὔτ᾽ ἀντ᾽ ἐμοῦ τέθνηκε, δὶς τόσως ἐμὲ
κτείνας ἀδελφῆς ζῶσαν. εἰ δ᾽ ἀμείψεται
φόνον δικάζων φόνος, ἀποκτενῶ σ᾽ ἐγὼ
καὶ παῖς Ὀρέστης πατρὶ τιμωρούμενοι·   1095
εἰ γὰρ δίκαι᾽ ἐκεῖνα, καὶ τάδ᾽ ἔνδικα.
[ὅστις δὲ πλοῦτον ἢ εὐγένειαν εἰσιδὼν
γαμεῖ πονηράν, μῶρός ἐστι· μικρὰ γὰρ
μεγάλων ἀμείνω σῶφρον᾽ ἐν δόμοις λέχη.

ΧΟΡΟΣ
    τύχη γυναικῶν ἐς γάμους. τὰ μὲν γὰρ εὖ,   1100
    τὰ δ᾽ οὐ καλῶς πίπτοντα δέρκομαι βροτῶν.]

ΚΛΥΤΑΙΜΗΣΤΡΑ
    ὦ παῖ, πέφυκας πατέρα σὸν στέργειν ἀεί·
    ἔστιν δὲ καὶ τόδ᾽· οἱ μέν εἰσιν ἀρσένων,
    οἳ δ᾽ αὖ φιλοῦσι μητέρας μᾶλλον πατρός.
    συγγνώσομαί σοι· καὶ γὰρ οὐχ οὕτως ἄγαν   1105
    χαίρω τι, τέκνον, τοῖς δεδραμένοις ἐμοί.
    σὺ δ᾽ ὧδ᾽ ἄλουτος καὶ δυσείματος χρόα
    λεχὼ νεογνῶν ἐκ τόκων πεπαυμένη;
    οἴμοι τάλαινα τῶν ἐμῶν βουλευμάτων·
    ὡς μᾶλλον ἢ χρῆν ἤλασ᾽ εἰς ὀργὴν πόσιν.   1110

ΗΛΕΚΤΡΑ
    ὀψὲ στενάζεις, ἡνίκ᾽ οὐκ ἔχεις ἄκη.
    πατὴρ μὲν οὖν τέθνηκε· τὸν δ᾽ ἔξω χθονὸς
    πῶς οὐ κομίζῃ παῖδ᾽ ἀλητεύοντα σόν;

ΚΛΥΤΑΙΜΗΣΤΡΑ
    δέδοικα· τοὐμὸν δ᾽, οὐχὶ τοὐκείνου, σκοπῶ.
    πατρὸς γάρ, ὡς λέγουσι, θυμοῦται φόνῳ.   1115

once you'd killed your husband, you didn't give
our father's home to us, but filled your bed
with someone else's goods and for a price   [1090]
bought yourself a marriage? And why is it
this husband has not been made an exile
for banishing your son? Why is he not dead
instead of me? The way I'm living now
has killed me twice as often as my sister.
If justice says that murder pays for murder,
your son Orestes and myself must kill you
to avenge our father. If your act was just,
then this one must be, too. Any man
watching out for wealth and noble birth
who gets married to a vicious woman
is a fool. A virtuous, humble marriage
is better for the home than something grand.

CHORUS LEADER

Marrying women is a matter of chance.   [1100]
Some, I notice, work out well, others badly.[29]

CLYTAEMNESTRA

My child, it was always in your nature
to love your father. That's how thing turn out.
Some are their fathers' children, while others
love their mothers rather than their fathers.
I'll forgive you. I don't get much delight,
my child, from what I've done. But why are you
so filthy, your body dressed in such poor clothes?
You've just been confined and given birth.[30]
Alas, my schemes have made me miserable!
I urged my anger on against my husband   [1110]
more than I should have.

ELECTRA

                    Well, it's too late now
to moan about it. There's no remedy.
My father's dead. But why don't you bring back
that exile from this land, your wandering son?

CLYTAEMNESTRA

I'm too afraid. I'm looking after me,
not him. And he's angry, so people say,
about the murder of his father.

ΗΛΕΚΤΡΑ

τί δαὶ πόσιν σὸν ἄγριον εἰς ἡμᾶς ἔχεις;

ΚΛΥΤΑΙΜΗΣΤΡΑ

τρόποι τοιοῦτοι· καὶ σὺ δ' αὐθάδης ἔφυς.

ΗΛΕΚΤΡΑ

ἀλγῶ γάρ· ἀλλὰ παύσομαι θυμουμένη.

ΚΛΥΤΑΙΜΗΣΤΡΑ

καὶ μὴν ἐκεῖνος οὐκέτ' ἔσται σοι βαρύς.

ΗΛΕΚΤΡΑ

φρονεῖ μέγ'· ἐν γὰρ τοῖς ἐμοῖς ναίει δόμοις.   1120

ΚΛΥΤΑΙΜΗΣΤΡΑ

ὁρᾷς; ἀν' αὖ σὺ ζωπυρεῖς νείκη νέα.

ΗΛΕΚΤΡΑ

σιγῶ· δέδοικα γάρ νιν ὡς δέδοικ' ἐγώ.

ΚΛΥΤΑΙΜΗΣΤΡΑ

παῦσαι λόγων τῶνδε. ἀλλὰ τί μ' ἐκάλεις, τέκνον;

ΗΛΕΚΤΡΑ

ἤκουσας, οἶμαι, τῶν ἐμῶν λοχευμάτων·
τούτων ὕπερ μοι θῦσον—οὐ γὰρ οἶδ' ἐγώ—   1125
δεκάτῃ σελήνῃ παιδὸς ὡς νομίζεται·
τρίβων γὰρ οὐκ εἴμ', ἄτοκος οὖσ' ἐν τῷ πάρος.

ΚΛΥΤΑΙΜΗΣΤΡΑ

ἄλλης τόδ' ἔργον, ἥ σ' ἔλυσεν ἐκ τόκων.

ΗΛΕΚΤΡΑ

αὐτὴ 'λόχευον κἄτεκον μόνη βρέφος.

ΚΛΥΤΑΙΜΗΣΤΡΑ

οὕτως ἀγείτων οἶκος ἵδρυται φίλων;   1130

ELECTRA
Why let your husband be so cruel to me?

CLYTAEMNESTRA
That's how he is. You've a stubborn nature.

ELECTRA
Because I'm suffering. But I'll stop being angry.

CLYTAEMNESTRA
Then he'll no longer behave harshly to you.

ELECTRA
He's got ideas of grandeur, living there   [1120]
inside my home.

CLYTAEMNESTRA
                    You see? Once again
you're kindling a new quarrel.

ELECTRA
                              I'll be silent,
my fear of him being what it is.

CLYTAEMNESTRA
                              Stop this talk.
Why have you sent for me, my child?

ELECTRA
You've heard, I think, that I have given birth.
Please offer up a sacrifice for me —
I don't know how to do that — on the tenth day,
as is our custom with an infant child.
I've had no children before this, and so
I lack experience.

CLYTAEMNESTRA
                    That task belongs
to the person who delivered the child.

ELECTRA
I was by myself in labour, so I bore
the child all on my own.

CLYTAEMNESTRA
                    Is this house here
so remote there are no friendly neighbours?   [1130]

101

Euripides

ΗΛΕΚΤΡΑ

πένητας οὐδεὶς βούλεται κτᾶσθαι φίλους.

ΚΛΥΤΑΙΜΗΣΤΡΑ

ἀλλ' εἶμι, παιδὸς ἀριθμὸν ὡς τελεσφόρον
θύσω θεοῖσι· σοὶ δ' ὅταν πράξω χάριν
τήνδ', εἶμ' ἐπ' ἀγρὸν οὗ πόσις θυηπολεῖ
Νύμφαισιν. ἀλλὰ τούσδ' ὄχους, ὀπάονες,   1135
φάτναις ἄγοντες πρόσθεθ'· ἡνίκ' ἂν δέ με
δοκῆτε θυσίας τῆσδ' ἀπηλλάχθαι θεοῖς,
πάρεστε· δεῖ γὰρ καὶ πόσει δοῦναι χάριν.

ΗΛΕΚΤΡΑ

χώρει πένητας ἐς δόμους· φρούρει δέ μοι
μή σ' αἰθαλώσῃ πολύκαπνον στέγος πέπλους.   1140
θύσεις γὰρ οἷα χρή σε δαίμοσιν θύη.
κανοῦν δ' ἐνῆρκται καὶ τεθηγμένη σφαγίς,
ἥπερ καθεῖλε ταῦρον, οὗ πέλας πεσῇ
πληγεῖσα· νυμφεύσῃ δὲ κἀν Ἅιδου δόμοις
ᾧπερ ξυνηῦδες ἐν φάει. τοσήνδ' ἐγὼ   1145
δώσω χάριν σοι, σὺ δὲ δίκην ἐμοὶ πατρός.

ΧΟΡΟΣ

ἀμοιβαὶ κακῶν· μετάτροποι πνέου-
σιν αὖραι δόμων. τότε μὲν ⟨ἐν⟩ λουτροῖς
   ἔπεσεν ἐμὸς ἐμὸς ἀρχέτας,
ἰάχησε δὲ στέγα λάινοί τε θριγκοὶ δόμων,   1150
   τάδ' ἐνέποντος· Ὦ σχέτλια· τί με, γύναι, φονεύσεις φίλαν
      πατρίδα δεκέτεσιν σποραῖσιν ἐλθόντ' ἐμάν;

ELECTRA

No one wants poor people as their friends.

CLYTAEMNESTRA

Well, I'll go and make the gods a sacrifice
for the full term of the child. When I'm done
carrying out this favour for you, I'll leave,
off to the field where my husband's offering
sacrifices to the Nymphs. You servants,
take this team away. Put them in the pens.
When you think I've finished sacrificing
to the gods, stand ready. I must satisfy
my husband's wishes, too.

ELECTRA

Enter this poor home.
For my sake take care the soot-stained walls   [1140]
don't stain your clothes. You'll give the gods
the sacrifice you ought to make.

[Clytaemnestra goes into the house]

And now
the basket's ready and the knife is keen,
the one which killed the bull you'll lie beside
when you're struck down. In Hades' home
you'll be wedded to the man you slept with
while you were alive. I'll be offering you
this favour, and you'll be giving me
retribution for my father.

[Electra goes into the house]

CHORUS

Evils are repaid. Winds of fortune
for this house are veering round.
Back then my leader, my very own,
fell murdered in his bath.
Roof and stone walls of the house   [1150]
resounded, echoing his cries—
"You vicious woman, why kill me
now I've come to my dear land
after ten harvest seasons?"[31]

παλίρρους δὲ τάνδ᾽ ὑπάγεται δίκαν 1155
διαδρόμου λέχους μέλεον, ἇ πόσιν
χρόνιον ἱκόμενον εἰς οἴκους
Κυκλώπειά τ᾽ οὐράνια τείχε᾽ ὀξυθήκτου βέλους
ἔκανεν αὐτόχειρ, πέλεκυν ἐν χεροῖν λαβοῦσ᾽· ἇ τλάμων
πόσις, ὅ τί ποτε τὰν τάλαιναν ἔσχεν κακόν; 1161
ὀρεία τις ὡς λέαιν᾽ ὀργάδων
δρύοχα νεμομένα, τάδε κατήνυσεν.

ΚΛΥΤΑΙΜΗΣΤΡΑ
ὦ τέκνα, πρὸς θεῶν, μὴ κτάνητε μητέρα. 1165

ΧΟΡΟΣ
κλύεις ὑπώροφον βοάν;

ΚΛΥΤΑΙΜΗΣΤΡΑ
ἰώ μοί μοι.

ΧΟΡΟΣ
ᾤμωξα κἀγὼ πρὸς τέκνων χειρουμένης.
νέμει τοι δίκαν θεός, ὅταν τύχῃ·
σχέτλια μὲν ἔπαθες, ἀνόσια δ᾽ εἰργάσω, 1170
τάλαιν᾽, εὐνέταν.

— ἀλλ᾽ οἵδε μητρὸς νεοφόνοις ἐν αἵμασι
πεφυρμένοι βαίνουσιν ἐξ οἴκων πόδα,
τροπαῖα δείγματ᾽ ἀθλίων προσφθεγμάτων.
οὐκ ἔστιν οὐδεὶς οἶκος ἀθλιώτερος
τῶν Τανταλείων οὐδ᾽ ἔφυ ποτ᾽ ἐκγόνων. 1175

ΟΡΕΣΤΗΣ
ἰὼ Γᾶ καὶ Ζεῦ πανδερκέτα
βροτῶν, ἴδετε τάδ᾽ ἔργα φόνι-
α μυσαρά, δίγονα σώματ᾽ ἐν
χθονὶ κείμενα πλαγᾷ 1180
χερὸς ὑπ᾽ ἐμᾶς, ἄποιν᾽ ἐμῶν
πημάτων.

The flow of justice has reversed itself
and brings to judgment for adultery
the killer of her unhappy husband
when he finally returned back home,
to the towering Cyclopean walls.
With her own hand she murdered him,
the sharpened edge of a keen axe
gripped in her fists. Poor sad husband!
What evils overtook this wretched woman?   [1160]
She did it like a mountain lion
prowling through a wooded meadow.

CLYTAEMNESTRA *[from inside the house]*
By the gods, children, don't kill your mother.

CHORUS
Do you hear that cry from inside the house?

CLYTAEMNESTRA *[screaming from inside]*
Ah . . . my god . . . ah . . . not me . . .

CHORUS
I moan, too, as her children beat her down.
The god indeed dispenses justice,
whenever it may come.
You've suffered horribly, sad lady,   [1170]
but you carried out unholy acts
against your husband.

*[Orestes, Pylades, and Electra and Attendants emerge slowly from the house
with the bodies of Aegisthus and Clytaemnestra]*

CHORUS LEADER
But here they come, moving from the house,
stained with fresh-spilt blood from their own mother,
a trophy, proof of their harsh sacrifice.
There is no house, not now or in the past,
more pitiable than the race of Tantalus.

ORESTES
O Earth and Zeus, who sees all mortal men,
look on these abominable and bloody acts,
these two corpses lying on the ground   [1180]
struck down by my hand, repayment
for everything I've suffered.

ΗΛΕΚΤΡΑ

δακρύτ᾽ ἄγαν, ὦ σύγγον᾽, αἰτία δ᾽ ἐγώ.
διὰ πυρὸς ἔμολον ἁ τάλαινα ματρὶ τᾷδ᾽,
ἅ μ᾽ ἔτικτε κούραν.

ΧΟΡΟΣ

ἰὼ τύχας, σᾶς τύχας,   1185
μᾶτερ τεκοῦσ᾽ ⟨ἄλαστα⟩,
ἄλαστα μέλεα καὶ πέρα
παθοῦσα σῶν τέκνων ὑπαί.
πατρὸς δ᾽ ἔτεισας φόνον δικαίως.

ΟΡΕΣΤΗΣ

ἰὼ Φοῖβ᾽, ἀνύμνησας δίκαι᾽   1190
ἄφαντα, φανερὰ δ᾽ ἐξέπρα-
ξας ἄχεα, φόνια δ᾽ ὤπασας
λάχε᾽ ἀπὸ γᾶς [τᾶς] Ἑλλανίδος.
τίνα δ᾽ ἑτέραν μόλω πόλιν;
τίς ξένος, τίς εὐσεβὴς   1195
ἐμὸν κάρα προσόψεται
ματέρα κτανόντος;

ΗΛΕΚΤΡΑ

ἰὼ ἰώ μοι. ποῖ δ᾽ ἐγώ, τίν᾽ ἐς χορόν,
τίνα γάμον εἶμι; τίς πόσις με δέξεται
νυμφικὰς ἐς εὐνάς;   1200

ΧΟΡΟΣ

πάλιν, πάλιν φρόνημα σὸν
μετεστάθη πρὸς αὔραν·
φρονεῖς γὰρ ὅσια νῦν, τότ᾽ οὐ
φρονοῦσα, δεινὰ δ᾽ εἰργάσω,
φίλα, κασίγνητον οὐ θέλοντα.   1205

ΟΡΕΣΤΗΣ

κατεῖδες, οἷον ἁ τάλαιν᾽ ἔξω πέπλων
ἔβαλεν, ἔδειξε μαστὸν ἐν φοναῖσιν,
ἰώ μοι, πρὸς πέδῳ
τιθεῖσα γόνιμα μέλεα; τὰν κόμαν δ᾽ ἐγώ . . .

ELECTRA

Too much cause to weep, my brother,
and I have made this happen.
In my wretchedness my fiery rage
burned on against my mother
who gave birth to me, her daughter.

CHORUS

Alas for fortune, for your fortune,
a mother who has given birth
to pain beyond enduring,
bearing wretched misery and more
from your own children, and yet it's just —
you've paid for murdering their father.   [1190]

ORESTES

Alas, Phoebus, that justice you sang of
had an obscure tone, but the pain you caused
was clear enough — you've given me
an exile's fate, far from these Greek lands.
To what other city can I go?
What host, what man with reverence
will look at me, who killed my mother?

ELECTRA

Alas, alas for me! Where do I go?
To what wedding or what choral dance?
What husband will take me to a bridal bed?   [1200]

CHORUS

Your spirit is shifting back once more
changing with the breeze. Your thoughts
are pious now, although profane before.
You've done dreadful things, my friend,
to your own reluctant brother.

ORESTES

Did you see that desperate woman,
how she threw her robe aside
and bared her breasts for slaughter?
Alas for me! The limbs which gave me birth
collapsing down onto the ground.
And her hair, I . . .

ΧΟΡΟΣ

    σάφ᾽ οἶδα, δι᾽ ὀδύνας ἔβας,   1210
    ἰήιον κλύων γόον
    ματρός, ἅ σ᾽ ἔτικτε.

ΟΡΕΣΤΗΣ

    βοὰν δ᾽ ἔλασκε τάνδε, πρὸς γένυν ἐμὰν
    τιθεῖσα χεῖρα· Τέκος ἐμόν, λιταίνω·   1215
    παρῄδων τ᾽ ἐξ ἐμᾶν
    ἐκρίμναθ᾽, ὥστε χέρας ἐμὰς λιπεῖν βέλος.

ΧΟΡΟΣ

    τάλαινα· πῶς ἔτλας φόνον
    δι᾽ ὀμμάτων ἰδεῖν σέθεν
    ματρὸς ἐκπνεούσας;   1220

ΟΡΕΣΤΗΣ

    ἐγὼ μὲν ἐπιβαλὼν φάρη κόραις ἐμαῖς
    φασγάνῳ κατηρξάμαν
    ματέρος ἔσω δέρας μεθείς.

ΗΛΕΚΤΡΑ

    ἐγὼ δ᾽ ἐπεγκέλευσά σοι
    ξίφους τ᾽ ἐφηψάμαν ἅμα.   1225

ΧΟΡΟΣ

    δεινότατον παθέων ἔρεξας.

ΟΡΕΣΤΗΣ

    λαβοῦ, κάλυπτε μέλεα ματέρος πέπλοις
    ⟨καὶ⟩ καθάρμοσον σφαγάς.
    φονέας ἔτικτες ἆρά σοι.

ΗΛΕΚΤΡΑ

    ἰδού, φίλᾳ τε κοὺ φίλᾳ   1230
    φάρεα τάδ᾽ ἀμφιβάλλομεν.

ΧΟΡΟΣ

    τέρμα κακῶν μεγάλων δόμοισιν.

CHORUS
                              I understand.   [1210]
    You had to go through torments,
    hearing your mother's screaming,
    the one who bore you.

ORESTES
    She stretched her hand toward my chin
    and cried, "My son, I beg you."
    She clung onto my cheeks—
    the sword dropped from my hands.

CHORUS
    Poor lady! How could you dare
    to watch your murdered mother
    breathe her last before your eyes.   [1220]

ORESTES
    I threw my cloak over my eyes,
    then sacrificed her with the sword.
    I shoved it in my mother's neck.

ELECTRA
    I was encouraging you—
    my hand was on the sword, as well.

CHORUS
    You have inflicted suffering
    of the most dreadful kind.

ORESTES
    Take this robe, hide our mother's limbs.
    Close up her wounds. You gave birth
    to your own murderers.

ELECTRA *[covering Clytaemnestra's corpse]*
    There, with this cloak I'm covering up   [1230]
    one who was loved and yet not loved.

CHORUS
    A end of the great troubles for this house.

[Castor and Polydeuces, the Dioscouri, appear above the building on the stage]

109

— ἀλλ' οἵδε δόμων ὑπὲρ ἀκροτάτων
φαίνουσι τίνες — δαίμονες ἢ θεῶν
τῶν οὐρανίων; οὐ γὰρ θνητῶν γ'   1235
ἥδε κέλευθος· τί ποτ' ἐς φανερὰν
ὄψιν βαίνουσι βροτοῖσιν;

ΔΙΟΣΚΟΥΡΟΙ

Ἀγαμέμνονος παῖ, κλῦθι· δίπτυχοι δέ σε
καλοῦσι μητρὸς σύγγονοι Διόσκοροι,
Κάστωρ κασίγνητός τε Πολυδεύκης ὅδε.   1240
δεινὸν δὲ ναὸς ἀρτίως πόντου σάλον
παύσαντ' ἀφίγμεθ' Ἄργος, ὡς ἐσείδομεν
σφαγὰς ἀδελφῆς τῆσδε, μητέρος δὲ σῆς.
δίκαια μέν νυν ἥδ' ἔχει, σὺ δ' οὐχὶ δρᾷς·
Φοῖβός τε, Φοῖβος — ἀλλ' ἄναξ γάρ ἐστ' ἐμός,   1245
σιγῶ· σοφὸς δ' ὢν οὐκ ἔχρησέ σοι σοφά.
αἰνεῖν δ' ἀνάγκη ταῦτα· τἀντεῦθεν δὲ χρὴ
πράσσειν ἃ Μοῖρα Ζεύς τ' ἔκρανε σοῦ πέρι.
Πυλάδῃ μὲν Ἠλέκτραν δὸς ἄλοχον ἐς δόμους,
σὺ δ' Ἄργος ἔκλιπ'· οὐ γὰρ ἔστι σοι πόλιν   1250
τήνδ' ἐμβατεύειν, μητέρα κτείναντι σήν.
δειναὶ δὲ κῆρές ⟨σ'⟩ αἱ κυνώπιδες θεαὶ
τροχηλατήσουσ' ἐμμανῆ πλανώμενον.
ἐλθὼν δ' Ἀθήνας Παλλάδος σεμνὸν βρέτας
πρόσπτυξον· εἴρξει γάρ νιν ἐπτοημένας   1255
δεινοῖς δράκουσιν ὥστε μὴ ψαύειν σέθεν,
γοργῶφ' ὑπερτείνουσα σῷ κάρᾳ κύκλον.
ἔστιν δ' Ἄρεώς τις ὄχθος, οὗ πρῶτον θεοὶ
ἕζοντ' ἐπὶ ψήφοισιν αἵματος πέρι,
Ἁλιρρόθιον ὅτ' ἔκταν' ὠμόφρων Ἄρης,   1260
μῆνιν θυγατρὸς ἀνοσίων νυμφευμάτων,
πόντου κρέοντος παῖδ', ἵν' εὐσεβεστάτη
ψῆφος βεβαία τ' ἐστὶν † ἔκ τε τοῦ † θεοῖς.
ἐνταῦθα καὶ σὲ δεῖ δραμεῖν φόνου πέρι.
ἴσαι δέ σ' ἐκσῴζουσι μὴ θανεῖν δίκῃ   1265
ψῆφοι τεθεῖσαι· Λοξίας γὰρ αἰτίαν
ἐς αὑτὸν οἴσει, μητέρος χρήσας φόνον.

CHORUS LEADER
But there above the roof beams of the house
something's coming. Spirits or gods from heaven?
That path does not belong to mortal men.
Why are they coming into human view?

DIOSCOURI *[from the top of the house]*[32]
Son of Agamemnon, you must listen.
The twin sons of Zeus are calling you,
Castor and his brother Polydeuces,   [1240]
your mother's brothers. We've just reached Argos,
after calming down a roaring storm at sea,
a dreadful threat to ships, after we had seen
the murder of our sister and your mother.
She's had justice, but you've not acted justly.
As for Phoebus, Phoebus, I'll say nothing.
He is my master. Although he's wise,
the prophecy he made to you was not.
You must accept these things and later on
act on what Fate and Zeus have set for you.
Give Electra to Pylades as his wife,
to take back home. And you must leave Argos.   [1250]
It's not right for you, who killed your mother,
to set foot in the city. The Keres,
those fearful dog-faced goddesses of death,
will hound you everywhere, a wanderer
in a mad fit.[33] You must go to Athens
and embrace Athena's sacred image.
She'll guard you from their dreadful writhing snakes
and stop them touching you, by holding out
her shield with the Gorgon's face above your head.
And there's the hill of Ares, where the gods
first sat down to cast their votes on bloodshed,
when savage Ares slaughtered Halirrothius,   [1260]
son of the god who rules the sea, enraged
at the unholy raping of his daughter.[34]
That place is where decisions made by vote
are most secure and sacred to the gods.
Here you must go on trial for murder.
The process will result in equal votes
so you'll be saved from death, for Apollo
will take responsibility himself.
His oracle advised your mother's murder.

καὶ τοῖσι λοιποῖς ὅδε νόμος τεθήσεται,
νικᾶν ἴσαις ψήφοισι τὸν φεύγοντ᾽ ἀεί.
δειναὶ μὲν οὖν θεαὶ τῷδ᾽ ἄχει πεπληγμέναι   1270
πάγον παρ᾽ αὐτὸν χάσμα δύσονται χθονός,
σεμνὸν βροτοῖσιν εὐσεβὲς χρηστήριον·
σὲ δ᾽ Ἀρκάδων χρὴ πόλιν ἐπ᾽ Ἀλφειοῦ ῥοαῖς
οἰκεῖν Λυκαίου πλησίον σηκώματος·
ἐπώνυμος δὲ σοῦ πόλις κεκλήσεται.   1275
σοὶ μὲν τάδ᾽ εἶπον· τόνδε δ᾽ Αἰγίσθου νέκυν
Ἄργους πολῖται γῆς καλύψουσιν τάφῳ.
μητέρα δὲ τὴν σὴν ἄρτι Ναυπλίαν παρὼν
Μενέλαος, ἐξ οὗ Τρωικὴν εἷλε χθόνα,
Ἑλένη τε θάψει· Πρωτέως γὰρ ἐκ δόμων   1280
ἥκει λιποῦσ᾽ Αἴγυπτον οὐδ᾽ ἦλθεν Φρύγας·
Ζεὺς δ᾽, ὡς ἔρις γένοιτο καὶ φόνος βροτῶν,
εἴδωλον Ἑλένης ἐξέπεμψ᾽ ἐς Ἴλιον.
Πυλάδης μὲν οὖν κόρην τε καὶ δάμαρτ᾽ ἔχων
Ἀχαιίδος γῆς οἴκαδ᾽ ἐσπορευέτω,   1285
καὶ τὸν λόγῳ σὸν πενθερὸν κομιζέτω
Φωκέων ἐς αἶαν καὶ δότω πλούτου βάρος·
σὺ δ᾽ Ἰσθμίας γῆς αὐχέν᾽ ἐμβαίνω ποδὶ
χώρει πρὸς ὄχθον Κεκροπίας εὐδαίμονα.
πεπρωμένην γὰρ μοῖραν ἐκπλήσας φόνου   1290
εὐδαιμονήσεις τῶνδ᾽ ἀπαλλαχθεὶς πόνων.

ΧΟΡΟΣ

ὦ παῖδε Διός, θέμις ἐς φθογγὰς
τὰς ὑμετέρας ἡμῖν πελάθειν;

ΔΙΟΣΚΟΥΡΟΙ

θέμις, οὐ μυσαραῖς τοῖσδε σφαγίοις.

ΗΛΕΚΤΡΑ

κἀμοὶ μύθου μέτα, Τυνδαρίδαι;   1295

This law will be established from then on —
those accused will always be acquitted
with equal votes. Struck by the pain of this,   [1270]
those fearful goddesses will then sink down
into a chasm right beside the hill,
a reverent and holy shrine for men.
You must settle an Arcadian city
by Alpheus' streams, near the sacred shrine
of Lycaean Apollo, and that city
will get its name from you. I'll tell you more.
As for Aegisthus' corpse, the citizens
in Argos here will place it in a grave.
But in your mother's case, Menelaus,
who's just arrived at Nauplia, so long
after he seized the territory of Troy,
will bury her, with Helen's help. She's come
from Proteus' home, leaving Egypt.
She never went to Troy. It was Zeus' wish
to stir up war and bloodshed among men.
So he sent Helen's image off to Troy.[35]
Since Pylades now has got a virgin wife,
let him go home and leave Achaean land,
with the man they call your brother-in-law
to the land of Phocis. He must give him
a great weight of riches. But as for you,
you must leave along the narrow Isthmus
and go to the blessed hill of Cecrops.[36]
Once you're completed your appointed fate   [1290]
for doing the murder, you'll find happiness
and be released from troubles.

CHORUS
      O sons of Zeus, are we permitted
      to come near and speak to you.

DIOSCOURI
      That is allowed — you're not defiled
      by this murder here.

ELECTRA
      And me, sons of Tyndareus,
      may I join in what's said?

Euripides

ΔΙΟΣΚΟΥΡΟΙ

καὶ σοί· Φοίβῳ τήνδ' ἀναθήσω
πρᾶξιν φονίαν.

ΧΟΡΟΣ

πῶς ὄντε θεὼ τῆσδέ τ' ἀδελφὼ
τῆς καπφθιμένης
οὐκ ἠρκέσατον κῆρας μελάθροις;   1300

ΔΙΟΣΚΟΥΡΟΙ

μοῖρά τ' ἀνάγκης ἦγ' ᾗ τὸ χρεών,
Φοίβου τ' ἄσοφοι γλώσσης ἐνοπαί.

ΗΛΕΚΤΡΑ

τίς δ' ἔμ' Ἀπόλλων, ποῖοι χρησμοὶ
φονίαν ἔδοσαν μητρὶ γενέσθαι;

ΔΙΟΣΚΟΥΡΟΙ

κοιναὶ πράξεις, κοινοὶ δὲ πότμοι,   1305
μία δ' ἀμφοτέρους
ἄτη πατέρων διέκναισεν.

ΟΡΕΣΤΗΣ

ὦ σύγγονέ μοι, χρονίαν σ' ἐσιδὼν
τῶν σῶν εὐθὺς φίλτρων στέρομαι
καὶ σ' ἀπολείψω σοῦ λειπόμενος.   1310

ΔΙΟΣΚΟΥΡΟΙ

πόσις ἔστ' αὐτῇ καὶ δόμος· οὐχ ἥδ'
οἰκτρὰ πέπονθεν, πλὴν ὅτι λείπει
πόλιν Ἀργείων.

ΗΛΕΚΤΡΑ

καὶ τίνες ἄλλαι στοναχαὶ μείζους
ἢ γῆς πατρίας ὅρον ἐκλείπειν;   1315

ΟΡΕΣΤΗΣ

ἀλλ' ἐγὼ οἴκων ἔξειμι πατρὸς
καὶ ἐπ' ἀλλοτρίαις ψήφοισι φόνον
μητρὸς ὑφέξω.

114

DIOSCOURI
    You may. It's to Apollo
    I ascribe this bloody act.

CHORUS
    How is that you two gods,
    brothers of this murdered woman,
    did not keep death's goddesses   [1300]
    far from her home?

DIOSCOURI
    Destiny and Fate brought what must be —
    and Apollo's unwise utterance.

ELECTRA
    What Apollo and what prophecies
    ordained that I must be
    my mother's murderer?

DIOSCOURI
    You worked together
    and shared a single fate.
    One ancestral curse
    has crushed you both.

ORESTES
    After such a lengthy time
    I've seen you, my sister,
    and immediately must lose   [1310]
    your love, abandoning you,
    as you abandon me.

DIOSCOURI
    She has a home and husband,
    and will not suffer piteously,
    except she leaves the Argives' city.

ELECTRA
    What else brings one more grief
    than moving out beyond the limits
    of one's native land?

ORESTES
    But I'll go from my father's house,
    then undergo a trial by strangers
    for murdering my mother.

ΔΙΟΣΚΟΥΡΟΙ

θάρσει· Παλλάδος
ὁσίαν ἥξεις πόλιν· ἀλλ᾽ ἀνέχου.　　　　1320

ΗΛΕΚΤΡΑ

περί μοι στέρνοις στέρνα πρόσαψον,
σύγγονε φίλτατε·
διὰ γὰρ ζευγνῦσ᾽ ἡμᾶς πατρίων
μελάθρων μητρὸς φόνιοι κατάραι.

ΟΡΕΣΤΗΣ

βάλε, πρόσπτυξον σῶμα· θανόντος δ᾽　　　　1325
ὡς ἐπὶ τύμβῳ καταθρήνησον.

ΔΙΟΣΚΟΥΡΟΙ

φεῦ φεῦ· δεινὸν τόδ᾽ ἐγηρύσω
καὶ θεοῖσι κλύειν.
ἔνι γὰρ κἀμοὶ τοῖς τ᾽ οὐρανίδαις
οἶκτοι θνητῶν πολυμόχθων.　　　　1330

ΟΡΕΣΤΗΣ

οὐκέτι σ᾽ ὄψομαι.

ΗΛΕΚΤΡΑ

οὐδ᾽ ἐγὼ ἐς σὸν βλέφαρον πελάσω.

ΟΡΕΣΤΗΣ

τάδε λοίσθιά μοι προσφθέγματά σου.

ΗΛΕΚΤΡΑ

ὦ χαῖρε, πόλις·
χαίρετε δ᾽ ὑμεῖς πολλά, πολίτιδες.　　　　1335

ΟΡΕΣΤΗΣ

ὦ πιστοτάτη, στείχεις ἤδη;

ΗΛΕΚΤΡΑ

στείχω βλέφαρον τέγγουσ᾽ ἁπαλόν.

116

DIOSCOURI
> Be brave. You'll reach
> Athena's sacred city.
> Just keep enduring all.

[1320]

ELECTRA
> Hold me, my dearest brother,
> your breast against my breast.
> The curses of a slaughtered mother
> divide us from our father's home.

ORESTES
> Throw your arms around me.
> Give me a close embrace.
> Then mourn for me as if I'd died,
> and you were at my burial mound.

DIOSCOURI
> Alas, alas! You've said things
> dreadful even for the gods to hear.
> I and those in heaven have pity
> for mortals who endure so much.

[1330]

ORESTES
> I'll not see you anymore.

ELECTRA
> I'll not come into your sight.

ORESTES
> These are the final words
> I'll ever say to you.

ELECTRA
> Farewell, my city! A long farewell
> to you my fellow countrywomen!

ORESTES
> Are you going already,
> my most faithful sister?

ELECTRA
> Yes, I'm leaving now
> my soft eyes wet with tears.

Euripides

ΟΡΕΣΤΗΣ

Πυλάδη, χαίρων ἴθι, νυμφεύου   1340
δέμας Ἠλέκτρας.

ΔΙΟΣΚΟΥΡΟΙ

τοῖσδε μελήσει γάμος· ἀλλὰ κύνας
τάσδ' ὑποφεύγων στεῖχ' ἐπ' Ἀθηνῶν·
δεινὸν γὰρ ἴχνος βάλλουσ' ἐπὶ σοὶ
χειροδράκοντες χρῶτα κελαιναί,   1345
δεινῶν ὀδυνῶν καρπὸν ἔχουσαι·
νὼ δ' ἐπὶ πόντον Σικελὸν σπουδῇ
σώσοντε νεῶν πρῴρας ἐνάλους.
διὰ δ' αἰθερίας στείχοντε πλακὸς
τοῖς μὲν μυσαροῖς οὐκ ἐπαρήγομεν,   1350
οἷσιν δ' ὅσιον καὶ τὸ δίκαιον
φίλον ἐν βιότῳ, τούτους χαλεπῶν
ἐκλύοντες μόχθων σῴζομεν.
οὕτως ἀδικεῖν μηδεὶς θελέτω
μηδ' ἐπιόρκων μέτα συμπλείτω·   1355
θεὸς ὢν θνητοῖς ἀγορεύω.

ΧΟΡΟΣ

χαίρετε· χαίρειν δ' ὅστις δύναται
καὶ ξυντυχίᾳ μή τινι κάμνει
θνητῶν, εὐδαίμονα πράσσει.

118

ORESTES

    Farewell, Pylades. Be happy.   [1340]
    Go and get married to Electra

DIOSCOURI

    The marriage will be their concern.
    You leave for Athens to escape these hounds,
    with their dark skins and hands made up of snakes.
    They're on a dreadful hunt to chase you down
    and bring you harvests of horrific pain.
    We two are off to the Sicilian sea.
    We'll hurry there to rescue ships at sea.
    As we pass through the flat expanse of air,
    we bring no help to those who've been defiled.   [1350]
    We do protect the men who way of their life
    reveres what's just and holy, releasing them
    from overbearing hardships. Let no one
    wish to act unjustly or to get on board
    with men who break their oaths. It's as a god
    that I address these words to mortal men.

[Castor and Polydeuces disappear. Orestes leaves the stage. Electra and Pylades move off in a different direction. The attendants go with them.]

CHORUS

    Farewell. Any mortal who can indeed fare well
    without being ground down by misfortune,
    that man will find his happiness.

[The Chorus carries the bodies back into the house]

NOTES

1. *Dardanus*: Ilion is an alternative name for Troy, and Dardanus is the name of a famous ancestor of Priam, king of Troy. Hence, the Trojans were often called Dardanians.

2. *ancient sceptre*: Tantalus was the legendary founder of the royal family of Argos, called the Pelopids after Tantalus' son Pelops. Tantalus was Agamemnon's and Menelaus' great-great-grandfather.

3. *totally disgraced*: Clytaemnestra's excuse for killing Agamemnon is, of course, the fact that he sacrificed their daughter Iphigeneia in order to enable the fleet to sail to Troy.

4. *still a virgin*: Cypris is a common name for Aphrodite, the goddess of sexual love. The name comes from the goddess' frequent association with Cyprus.

5. *a water jug*: the shaven head may be a token of mourning or a sign of Electra's low status now or both.

6. *couch of death*: Agamemnon was killed in his bath, trapped under his cloak, as if under a hunting net.

7. *your house, as well*: Helen and Clytaemnestra were twin sisters born to Leda, but with different fathers—Tyndareus, king of Sparta and Leda's husband, wasClytaemnestra's father, but Zeus, who in the form of a swan raped Leda, was Helen's.

8. *Castor*: Castor and Polydeuces (also called Pollux), the Dioscuri, were twin brothers of Helen and Clytaemnestra, all born at the same time to Leda, queen of Sparta (hence Castor is an uncle of Electra). Polydeuces and Helen were children of Zeus, while Castor and Clytaemnestra were children of Tyndareus. When Castor was killed (before the Trojan war), Polydeuces turned down immortality, but Zeus allowed them to alternate, living among the gods and men, changing each day.

9. *oracles of Loxias*: Loxias is another name for Apollo, the god whose shrine Orestes consults before coming to Argos (as he mentions at line 115 above). But we do not know the text of the oracle (although

we later learn it encouraged him to commit the revenge murders), and Electra is, one assumes, ignorant of Orestes' visit to the shrine.

10. *Nereids*: These are sea goddesses, daughters of Nereus. Achilles' mother, Thetis, was one of them.

11. *sons of Atreus*: These lines refer to the centaur Chiron (or Cheiron), half man and half horse, who in the region described, educated Achilles and other heroes. Pelion and Ossa are two famous mountains. Hephaestus is the god who made Achilles' divine armour (at the request of Achilles' mother, the goddess Thetis) after his own armour worn by Patroclus had been captured by Hector, the leader of the Trojan forces.

12. *Maia's country child*: Perseus was the hero who killed Medusa, the most ferocious of the Gorgons (her face turned men to stone). Hermes, divine son of Zeus, assisted Perseus in the exploit. He is called a "country child" because he is associated with farming and hunting.

13. *racing lioness*: This is a reference to the monster Chimaera, a fire-breathing lioness with a goat's body and head growing out of its back. The Chimaera was killed by the hero Bellerophon. The reference to Hector is a reminder that he had to face Achilles' shield in his final and fatal encounter with Achilles (described in Book 22 of the *Iliad*).

14. *slipped past the guard*: This line is corrupt and makes little sense in the Greek. The words "someone slipped past the guard" have been put in to make sense of Electra's words, turning the line into a suggestion that some citizen may have eluded Aegisthus' sentries and paid a tribute to Agamemnon. As Cropp points out, omitting the line makes it read as if the Old Man is interrupting Electra, a dramatically implausible action.

15. *Thyestes' son*: Aegisthus is the son of Thyestes (brother of Agamemnon's father, Atreus). Atreus and Thyestes quarreled, and Atreus killed Thyestes' sons and served to him at dinner. Aegisthus survived the slaughter or (in other accounts) was born after the notorious banquet. Euripides' play makes no direct mention of this important part of the traditional story.

16. *I'll accept those words*: Cropp suggests that Orestes' rather odd phraseology in this speech and the previous one stems from the fact that he

is using the language of ritual, as if he were consulting an oracle, first hoping that he gets a good pronouncement which he can understand and then accepting the "utterance."

17. *some new birth*: the Nymphs, minor country goddesses, were associated with physical health, including childbirth and childhood.

18. *ten days ago*: the "quarantine," Cropp notes, was a period immediately after childbirth in which the mother was kept in seclusion to avoid contamination.

19. *be a man*: There is some confusion and argument about the allocation and position of this line, which in the Greek comes after this speech of Electra's and is divided between Orestes and Electra. I have followed Cropp's suggestion and given the entire line to Electra at the beginning of her speech to Orestes.

20. *fleece of gold*: Thyestes and Atreus were brothers who quarreled. Thyestes seduced Atreus' wife, Aerope, and, in revenge, Atreus killed Thyestes' sons and served them up to him for dinner. Aegisthus is Thyestes' surviving son. The golden lamb in question seems to be the symbol of the right to rule in Mycenae.

21. *Ammon's land*: This is a reference to North Africa, where Ammon's shrine was located.

22. *glorious brothers*: Clytaemnestra's brothers are Castor and Polydeuces, or Pollux, the Dioscuri, twin brothers of Helen and Clytaemnestra, all born at the same time to Leda, queen of Sparta (hence Castor is an uncle of Electra). Polydeuces and Helen were children of Zeus, while Castor and Clytaemnestra were children of Tyndareus. When Castor was killed (before the Trojan war), Polydeuces turned down immortality, but Zeus allowed them to alternate, living among the gods and men, changing each day.

23. *Alpheus*: Cropp suggests that this is a reference to the Olympic games.

24. *Phoebus* is a common name for Apollo, the god whose oracle Orestes consulted before coming to Argos. The god advised him to carry out the revenge murders.

25. *noble twins*: This is another reference to Castor and Polydeuces (or Pollux) twin brothers of Clytaemnestra. Strictly speaking only one of them was a child of Zeus (as was Helen, Clytaemnestra's sister). Clytaemnestra and Castor were children of Tyndareus. The twins

occupied a position among the stars (we call them the Gemini), and hence were an aid to navigation.

26. *the child I lost*: This is a reference to Clytaemnestra's daughter Iphigeneia, whom Agamemnon sacrificed at the start of the Trojan expedition in order to persuade the gods to change the winds so that the fleet could sail. Clytaemnestra gives details of the story in her next long speech.

27. *Aulis*: This was the agreed meeting point for the great naval expedition to Troy. Bad winds delayed the fleet for so long that the entire enterprise was jeopardized. The gods demanded a sacrifice from Agamemnon.

28. *in the same house*: The young girl was Cassandra, daughter of Priam, king of Troy, given as a war prize to Agamemnon. She was a prophetess under a divine curse: she always spoke the truth, but no one ever believed her. She is an important character in Aeschylus' treatment of this story in his play *Agamemnon*.

29. *others badly*: These lines of pithy moralizing at the end of Electra's speech and in this speech by the Chorus Leader sound very out of place here. Some editors have removed them as a later addition to the text.

30. *given birth*: Some editors find these two and half lines a very odd change of subject for Clytaemnestra, who is now dwelling on her own sorrow. Cropp moves them to the opening of Clytaemnestra's speech at 1380 below, where they do seem more appropriate.

31. *harvest times*: At this point in the manuscript two lines appear to be missing.

32. *DIOSCOURI*: It is not clear which of the twin brothers speaks to the human characters or whether they alternate or speak together.

33. *mad fit*. The Keres are the children of Night, death spirits who prey on living human beings. Although they are different from the Furies (who chase down those who have committed murder in the family), here their function seems quite similar.

34. *of his daughter*: Ares, son of Zeus and god of war, killed Poseidon's son, Halirrothius, over the attempted rape of Ares' daughter, Alcippe. Ares was put on trial on Olympus and acquitted by the gods.

35. *off to Troy*: In Homer's account (in the *Odyssey*) Menelaus and Helen
     take a long time to get home from Troy, being blown off course and
     spending a few years in Egypt. Proteus is the Old Man of the Sea,
     who helps Menelaus in Egypt. The story of Helen's being detained in
     Egypt on her way to Troy and never going to the city at all is not in
     Homer's epic, but was known before Euripides makes use of it here
     and in his play *Helen*.

36. *blessed hill of Cecrops*: The Isthmus is the Isthmus of Corinth, a nar-
     row strip of land joining the Peloponnese (where Argos is situated)
     with the main part of Greece. Cecrops is the mythical first king and
     founder of Athens. The Cecropian Hill is a reference to the Acropolis
     in Athens.

28604519R00077

Printed in Great Britain
by Amazon